P9-CCU-562

NEW TESTAMENT MESSAGE

A Biblical-Theological Commentary

Wilfrid Harrington, O.P. and Donald Senior, C.P.
EDITORS

New Testament Message, Volume 13

EPHESIANS

Lionel Swain

Michael Glazier, Inc.
Wilmington, Delaware

MICHAEL GLAZIER, INC.
1210A King Street
Wilmington, Delaware 19801

©1980 by Michael Glazier, Inc.
All rights reserved.

Library of Congress Catalog Card Number: 80-68226
International Standard Book Number
New Testament Message series: 0-89453-123-9
EPHESIANS: 0-89453-136-0

The Bible text in this publication is from the Revised Standard Version of the Bible, copyrighted 1946, 1952, ©1971, 1973 by the Division of Christian Education of the National Council of the Churches of Christ in the U.S.A., and used by permission.

Printed in the United States of America by Abbey Press

CONTENTS

Editors' Preface   vii

Introduction   ix

Address and Greeting. 1:1-2   1

Prayer. 1:3 - 3:21   4

Blessing. 1:3-14   5

The Plan of Salvation in General. 1:3-10   6
Blessing. 1:3   6
Choice. 1:4   9
Destiny. 1:5-6   10
Redemption. 1:7-8   16
Revelation. 1:9-10   19

The Union of Jews and Gentiles. 1:11-14   25

Excursus.   29
The Father   29
The Lord Jesus Christ   34
The Holy Spirit   39
The Trinity   43

Thanksgiving. 1:15-16   45

Intercession. 1:17-19   47

Description of God's Power. 1:20 - 2:10   48

In Christ. 1:20-23   48
In Believers. 2:1-10   51

The Union of Jews and Gentiles. 2:11-22   56

    The Situation Before Christ. 2:11-12   56
    Christ's Unifying Work. 2:13-18   56
    The Present Situation. 2:19-22   59

Intercession. 3:1-19   64

Excursus.   70
    Gospel.   70
    Faith.   72

Doxology. 3:20-21   75

Exhortation. 4:1 - 6:20   77

    Excursus: Christian Behaviour   78

    Exhortation To All Believers. 4:1 - 5:20   82

    Exhortation To Particular Categories of
    Believers. 5:21 - 6:9   93

    Exhortation To All The Faithful. 6:10-20   103

Personal News. 6:21-22   110

Final Greeting. 6:23-24   111

Postword   112

Further Reading   114

EDITORS' PREFACE

New Testament Message is a commentary series designed to bring the best of biblical scholarship to a wide audience. Anyone who is sensitive to the mood of the church today is aware of a deep craving for the Word of God. This interest in reading and praying the scriptures is not confined to a religious elite. The desire to strengthen one's faith and to mature in prayer has brought Christians of all types and all ages to discover the beauty of the biblical message. Our age has also been heir to an avalanche of biblical scholarship. Recent archaeological finds, new manuscript evidence, and the increasing volume of specialized studies on the Bible have made possible a much more profound penetration of the biblical message. But the flood of information and its technical nature keeps much of this scholarship out of the hands of the Christian who is eager to learn but is not a specialist. *New Testament Message* is a response to this need.

The subtitle of the series is significant: "A Biblical-Theological Commentary." Each volume in the series, while drawing on up-to-date scholarship, concentrates on bringing to the fore in understandable terms the specific message of each biblical author. The essay-format (rather than a word-by-word commentary) helps the reader savor the beauty and power of the biblical message and, at the same time, understand the sensitive task of responsible biblical interpretation.

A distinctive feature of the series is the amount of space given to the "neglected" New Testament writings, such as Colossians, James, Jude, the Pastoral Letters, the Letters of Peter and John. These briefer biblical books make a significant but often overlooked contribution to the richness of the New Testament. By assigning larger than normal coverage to these books, the series hopes to give these parts of Scripture the attention they deserve.

Because *New Testament Message* is aimed at the entire English speaking world, it is a collaborative effort of international proportions. The twenty-two contributors represent biblical scholarship in North America, Britain, Ireland and Australia. Each of the contributors is a recognized expert in his or her field, has published widely, and has been chosen because of a proven ability to communicate at a popular level. And, while all of the contributors are Roman Catholic, their work is addressed to the Christian community as a whole. The New Testament is the patrimony of all Christians.It is the hope of all concerned with this series that it will bring a fuller appreciation of God's saving Word to his people.

Wilfrid Harrington, O.P.
Donald Senior, C.P.

INTRODUCTION

Author, Destination, Occasion, Date

ALTHOUGH THE AUTHOR of our letter clearly presents himself as the apostle Paul, there is today no unanimity among scholars about his identity. Since the middle of the last century considerable doubt has been cast on the Pauline authorship, mainly because of the very close similarities between this letter and that to the Colossians, but also because of the marked differences in language, style and thought between this and those letters which are generally recognised as Pauline.

Scholars are almost equally divided on the point, and both camps number highly respectable names. This fact alone is sufficient indication that the case against Pauline authorship is not proven. It also legitimizes the assumption maintained throughout the present commentary that Paul was in fact the author, at least in the sense that he was responsible for its main ideas. It may be that in this case greater latitude was given to his secretary than in other instances. This hypothesis could account for the curious admixture of similarities and differences just mentioned.

There is general agreement among scholars, however, that this letter was not addressed originally to the church at Ephesus. The title "to the Ephesians" is a later addition and the phrase "in Ephesus" in 1:1 is absent both from the best manuscripts and the earliest patristic quotations. The author also gives the impression that he is not personally acquainted with his readers – which would hardly be the case if he were addressing the faithful among whom he had worked for about three years (Acts 20:31). The likelihood is that this letter was originally a circular letter destined for several churches.

At the time of writing the author is clearly in prison. If the author is Paul, three main imprisonments come to mind: in Ephesus, in Caesarea, in Rome, the first being surmised, the other two established. The most likely candidate is Rome, given the similarities between Ephesians and Colossians. In this case, our letter would have emanated from Paul's first Roman "house arrest" sometime during the period 61-63.

Ephesians is unique in the Pauline corpus in that it does not betray the occasion for which it was written. Again, the close similarities with Colossians might suggest a common occasion. But Ephesians does not evince the polemics of the Colossians crisis. It has been reasonably suggested that in Ephesians Paul took up the insights which he had gained in the Colossians crisis and reviewed his ideas of the Christ-event serenely in their light. Thus Ephesians would bear basically the same relationship to Colossians as does Romans to Galatians.

Literary Form and Structure

Apart from the address and greeting (1:1-2) and the last four verses (6:21-24), Ephesians does not appear like a letter at all. It is more like a treatise or homily in the guise of a letter. Apart from the passages just mentioned, it is clearly composed of two parts, of almost identical length: 1:3-3:21 and 4:1-6:20. The first part, which could be called the "doctrinal" section, is in fact made up entirely of prayers. The second part – the "moral" section – is a series of exhortations. Both of these sections contain elements which reflect the early church's baptismal liturgy. Ephesians appears, therefore, as a very carefully constructed amalgam of prayers and homiletic elements. The first three chapters concentrate on the Christ-event considered "objectively", while the last three concentrate on the faithful's acceptance of this event.

The Message

In the first main part of Ephesians Paul emphasises above all the loving initiative of God the Father in the work of salvation. This salvation is the object of the Father's eternal plan. It is centred in Christ who has the cosmic role of mediating the recapitulation of the whole universe. Thus redemption is now seen to involve not only people but also the whole of creation. This view of salvation renders obsolete the division of humanity into two groups: the Jews and the Gentiles. All people are now united in Christ.

If redemption concerns the whole cosmos, it concerns the church in a particular way. The church is the body of Christ, that is his visible and tangible presence in the cosmos.

By baptism we participate in the saving mystery of Christ's death, resurrection and heavenly exaltation and become members of Christ's body. By the same experience we form one people, one "man", one living temple in the Spirit. Thus the work of salvation is "Trinitarian": God the Father saves the universe in Christ, through the Spirit.

In the second main part Paul stresses the need for the baptised to correspond to, and co-operate with, God's initiative and immanent activity, although it is clear that even this behaviour on our part is, in reality, God's action within us.

The Christ-event, appropriated in baptism, has repercussions in all the areas of human life, particularly within the church where it is the motive of unity and harmony between the different members of Christ's body. In general, it requires a complete renewal of behaviour, tantamount to a new creation. It affects people in all the dimensions of their social life. They are now called to lead their family life, of husbands, wives, parents, children, masters and slaves in the light of Christ.

The faithful are not only the beneficiaries of salvation; they are also its instruments, invested with the power of Christ. For, although God's saving plan has been realised initially in Christ, it has still to be fully accomplished in his members and in the universe.

Prayer, especially intercessory prayer, has an important role to play in the faithful's salvific work. Paul the apostle gives them an example in this regard in the first part of his letter. It is by prayer that the faithful open themselves to Christ's power and so participate in God's saving love for the universe. It is in fact love that is at the beginning and the end of God's plan for the cosmos. God saves the world out of love and we live the reality of this salvation by loving one another.

ADDRESS AND GREETING.
1:1-2.

> **1** Paul, an apostle of Christ Jesus by the will of God,
> To the saints who are also faithful in Christ Jesus:
> [2]Grace to you and peace from God our Father and the
> Lord Jesus Christ.

FROM THE VERY BEGINNING, the author clearly presents himself as the apostle Paul and, as was mentioned above, the critics have been unable to adduce convincing proof against Paul's authorship of this letter. As in Galatians, Romans (and the Pastorals), Paul does not associate any of his collaborators with himself in the writing of his letter. This could be an indication of its impersonal and general character. These opening words are more than a formality. As usual, Paul uses his address and greeting to introduce some of the major themes which he will develop throughout his letter. He stresses that he is "an apostle of Christ Jesus" – the role which he has had to defend previously, especially in Galatians. Later in this letter he will describe this role more serenely. For the moment he insists that he is an apostle "by the will of God", applying to his own vocation what is probably the most important and profound theme of the whole work: the completely uninvited initiative of God in the achievement of our salvation.

Paul's role as an apostle is an essential part of this saving work. Those whom Paul addresses are "saints" in so far as they have been sanctified or consecrated through Christ's saving work which they have appropriated by baptism. All the baptised, because they are "in Christ Jesus", are "saints", sharing as they do in Christ's holiness. The phrase "in Christ Jesus" announces another major theme of the letter: the mediation of Christ. If our salvation has its origin in God, it is realised only *in* Christ. It is only *in* him that Christians are holy. Likewise, it is only *in* him that they are "faithful". Although "saints" describes the Christians' "objective" condition and "faithful" their fidelity to this God-given condition, it is remarkable that this fidelity is something other than mere human response to God's initiative. Like holiness, it is possible only *in* Christ. Even loyalty to God is part of his saving work which, originating in him, is achieved in Christ. It is striking, however, that, in the very first verse of this letter, Paul evokes the two aspects of God's saving work – what we would call the "objective" and the "subjective" – which will receive distinct treatment in the two main parts of the letter.

With the mention of "grace" and "peace" Paul also introduces two important themes of the letter. The "grace" which Paul does not merely wish for his readers but, rather, is the object of his most ardent prayer, is the completely unmerited favour which God has already bestowed upon mankind in Christ. Likewise, the "peace" is not just a cessation or absence of hostility. It is the reality expressed by the Hebrew word – itself a greeting – "*shalom*", which means a plentitude of everything that is good. As we shall see later, it is Paul's contention that this true peace has been realised already by God in and through Christ. If he now prays for it to be given to his readers, this is not as if it has to be wrested by intercession from the hands of an unwilling or insensitive God. It is because he wishes his readers to become aware of the gift which God, in his own loving, paternal initiative has already made to them. It is they who are to be changed by this prayer, not God. As Paul has already suggested (v.1), this "grace" and "peace" – the reality of our salvation – originate in God. Now he stresses the loving initiative of God by referring to him as "our Father". For Paul God is not merely the unique omnipotent creator of the universe. He is also – and first and foremost – "our Father", that is the father of all men, Jews and Gentiles alike. This fatherhood has its basis not in a natural generative act, but in the new birth which God has made possible for all mankind through faith and baptism in his unique Son, Jesus Christ. It is in this sense that Paul speaks of the "grace" and "peace" coming to us also from "the Lord Jesus Christ". The basic confession of faith, made at baptism, is precisely that Jesus is the Christ and Lord. To accept Jesus Christ really as "Lord" is to submit oneself to him, as a servant to a master, to acknowledge him as the main inspiration of one's life. This commitment is what the New Testament means by faith. Although Paul does not refer to Jesus as "God" and, indeed, stresses that our salvation is achieved in and through Jesus, he nevertheless ascribes a "divine" character to him, in so far as he calls him "Lord". This term is a translation of God's divine name – Yahweh – in the Old Testament. Thus, if for Paul God is Father, Jesus is also "God", in the sense that he shares the prerogatives of Yahweh. He does this as "Son", that is as the one who receives all that he has and is from the Father. This is why, by committing himself to Jesus in faith and baptism, the Christian becomes a beneficiary of the salvation which has been achieved in the Son – in other words, becomes a sharer in Christ's life and a son of God. Faith is the expression, the articulation and the realisation of our divine sonship "in Christ Jesus" (v.1).

PRAYER.
1:3 – 3:21

THE ADDRESS and greeting, together with the item of personal news (6:21-22) and the final greeting (6:23-24), is the only indication that Ephesians is a letter in the strict sense of this term. Divested of these sections, the work appears more like a homily or sermon, the kind of address which might well have been delivered to the recently baptised – perhaps even on the very occasion of their baptism. Certainly baptismal motifs abound throughout this letter.

The first part of the homily is in the form of a long series of prayers of different kinds: 1:3-14: blessing; 1:15-16: thanksgiving: 1:17-2:22: intercession; 3:1-19: intercession; 3:20-21: doxology. This fact suggests a liturgical origin or background. The second part is in the form of a series of exhortations: 4:1-5:20; 5:21-6:9; 6:10-20, all of which would be perfectly appropriate in a homily directed to neophytes. Indeed, it could be said that the whole of the body of Ephesians is both prayer and exhortation, in so far as the "exhortation" section is nothing more or less than "prayer" addressed to the readers, while the "prayer" section, being – as we have seen (v.2) – more for the benefit of the readers than for God's ears, is really implicit "exhortation".

Blessing.

1:3-14.

[3]Blessed be the God and Father of our Lord Jesus Christ, who has blessed us in Christ with every spiritual blessing in the heavenly places, [4]even as he chose us in him before the foundation of the world, that we should be holy and blameless before him. [5]He destined us in love to be his sons through Jesus Christ, according to the purpose of his will, [6]to the praise of his glorious grace which he freely bestowed on us in the Beloved. [7]In him we have redemption through his blood, the forgiveness of our trespasses, according to the riches of his grace [8]which he lavished upon us. [9]For he has made known to us in all wisdom and insight the mystery of his will, according to his purpose which he set forth in Christ [10]as a plan for the fullness of time, to unite all things in him, things in heaven and things on earth.

[11]In him, according to the purpose of him who accomplishes all things according to the counsel of his will, [12]we who first hoped in Christ have been destined and appointed to live for the praise of his glory. [13]In him you also, who have heard the word of truth, the gospel of your salvation, and have believed in him, were sealed with the promised Holy Spirit, [14]which is the guarantee of our inheritance until we acquire possession of it, to the praise of his glory.

The first of the series of prayers is a "blessing", modelled on the Jewish *berakah*, associated particularly with meals. Indeed, both the style and the main themes of this blessing are thoroughly Jewish and, with the obvious exception of the explicit references to Christ, can be paralleled from Jewish literature, particularly the writings of the Qumran community. The most important characteristic of the "blessing" genre is that it is responsive. It is a "blessing" of God in response to his previous "blessing" of his creation.

Properly speaking, only God can and does "bless", because to "bless" means to give what is good and God alone is the source of goodness. When in the Bible (e.g. Gen 27:27-29) one man "blesses" another, this is only to invoke God's blessing upon him. When a man "blesses" God (e.g. Ps 96:2) he recognises, acknowledges, God as the source of his happiness and implicitly thanks him for it. Frequently the blessing will detail the different aspects of God's gift. Thus it also serves as a profession of faith. The "blessing" of Ephesians mentions most of the major themes found in the rest of the work and can be read as a veritable résumé or synthesis. We have already seen that Paul packs as much of his message as he can even into his address and greeting (vv.1-2). In the "blessing" he has more room to expand his thoughts. It is remarkable that, throughout the rest of the work, he will frequently return to the ideas which he has expressed in this "blessing". Being an excellent teacher, he knew how to inculcate his message by reiterating it in different literary forms and presenting it from different angles. It remains true, however, that the essence of this message is contained in this first prayer.

THE PLAN OF SALVATION IN GENERAL.
1:3-10.

The inaugural "blessing" clearly has two parts: vv.3-10 and vv.11-14. In the first part, expressed in one long and complicated sentence –one of the longest in the New Testament – Paul describes enthusiastically what we have learnt to call the "plan of salvation" in general, that is as it refers to all men. In the second part, having paused to take breath, he concentrates on one particular aspect of this plan: the union of Jews and Gentiles which it was designed to achieve.

Blessing.
1:3.

> [3]Blessed be the God and Father of our Lord Jesus Christ, who has blessed us in Christ with every spiritual blessing in the heavenly places.

At the beginning of this prayer Paul strikes a note of cheerfulness and optimism. A "blessing", of its very nature, springs from the recognition of the good things of life seen as blessings from God. Paul's cheerfulness is all the more remarkable in that he is ostensibly writing from prison. From this prison he prays aloud and assumes that his hearers and readers both already share the same basic religious experience and are disposed to developing this experience further. Without this assumption, Ephesians can have no message. It is indeed Paul who prays here, but he prays as the representative of a community, recalling what God has done for "us" and praising him for it. The prayer is addressed to "the God and Father of our Lord Jesus Christ". As in v.2, Paul distinguishes very clearly between God and Jesus Christ. In recognising Jesus as Lord (in the sense which we have already seen), Paul and his community must necessarily accept *his* God and Father as *their* God and Father (cf. Jn 20:17). It is the God of Jesus Christ, that is the God who has revealed himself in Christ to be Father, who is "blessed" because of the blessings which he, precisely as Father, has bestowed upon mankind in Christ. Christ's mission was to mediate both the reality and the knowledge of these blessings. To acknowledge him as Lord, therefore, involves recognising God as Father, that is as the One who, of his very nature, blesses, gives, loves – is, indeed, love itself (cf. 1 Jn 4:8). The prayer of blessing is not only an expression of cheerfulness, it is also a profession of faith in God as love.

This blessing of God, with all the joy and happiness which it expresses, is inspired by, and is in response to, God's previous acknowledged blessings bestowed on us in Christ. For Paul the Christ-event is decidedly a "blessing", a good thing for mankind. He also considers that all of God's blessings have been given to us *in* Christ. Not only does he refer explicitly to "every spiritual blessing", but he also uses the expresson "in Christ" or its equivalent ten times throughout the blessing. He maintains that if we understand Christ correctly we cannot but see him as "good news" for mankind. It is in him, that is in the revelation of God and man which he represents, that mankind will find its ultimate fulfilment and happiness.

Paul describes the blessings which God has bestowed on mankind in Christ as "spiritual". This term should not be understood as opposed to "material", as if Paul considered God's blessings as not involving man's real world. In the first place, it is very probably an allusion to the Holy Spirit who is received at baptism (v.13). Thus the first verse of this prayer contains a reference to the Trinity of God (the Father), Christ and the Spirit. Moreover, this Holy Spirit is precisely the spirit of the promise (v.13). Mention of the promise evokes (especially in the context of a Jewish *berakah*) the blessings promised to the father of the Jews, Abraham (cf. Gen 12:2-3), culminating in the blessing of all the nations in Abraham: "and in you all the families of the earth shall be blessed" (Gen 12:3). The "spiritual" character of this promise made to Abraham derives not from its concern with spiritual as opposed to material benefits (such a dichotomy would be alien to the biblical view of reality anyway), but from the way in which the promise is fulfilled, that is not according to what we would call the "natural course of events". Thus the births of Isaac and Jacob were spiritual, as was the latter's inheritance of the promise. What Paul is suggesting in his prayer is that the "spiritual" promise made to Abraham has been fully realised in Christ, the true "spiritual" seed of Abraham (cf. Gal 3:16). Indeed, the designation of God as Father also suggests that the real father to whom all people (and not only the Jews) should look is not Abraham but God himself. This relationship of all people to God as Father establishes the true brotherhood of mankind, a unity which heals the disharmony among men caused by the Tower of Babel incident (cf. Gen 11:1-9) and which the call of Abraham (cf. Gen 12:1-3) was supposed to rectify. The "spiritual" nature of the blessing which God has made to the world in Christ is assured by the way it has been conferred: "in the heavenly places". It is by his extraordinary resurrection and ascension into heaven that Christ has become the complete mediator of God's blessing. By introducing Christ – the eldest brother – into the full realisation of his presence (mythically represented by "heaven"), God has potentially introduced all other men to this blessing. According to Paul, the unique endeavour of the newly baptised should be to "realise" – in the double sense of both understanding and making real – this potentiality in their ordinary daily lives. In this way the "spiritual" blessing runs no risk of being identified with "pie in the sky when you die". As Paul will make clear in the second main part of his homily, the blessing which he has in mind has an immediate concern and involves the more mundane aspects of human life.

Choice.
1:4.

> ⁴even as he chose us in him before the foundation of the world, that we should be holy and blameless before him.

Paul now begins to describe God's blessing in greater detail. Having just (v.3) drawn attention to the final point of this blessing: the heavenly places, he first of all recalls its starting point: God's choice of us "before the foundation of the world". Just as the history of Israel's blessing begins with a choice: God's choice of Abraham, so our blessing begins with a choice which emphasizes God's initiative in our regard (cf. v.1). Being a beneficiary of God's blessing bears no relationship to what we are of ourselves or to what we have done. God's blessing, like his choice, is not a reward. It is solely the effect of God's loving benevolence. In our case, this choice originates not with Abraham but before Abraham, indeed, "before the foundation of the world". With this insight Paul shifts the focal point of God's choice from Israel, where (cf. Rom 9-11) he had previously considered it to be, to creation itself. According to his present perspective, we become beneficiaries of God's blessing not simply because we become members of the people of Israel or, even, because we have had transferred to us the privileges which were once the prerogatives of this people but because we (whether or not we were once members of the people of Israel) have been chosen before the foundation of the world. Paul has passed through the anguish expressed in Rom 8-11 over the role of Israel in the history of salvation only to realise, as he now intimates in Ephesians, that Israel has no essential role at all. Being saved depends uniquely upon God's choice made before the existence of Israel. By this very fact, this choice is not exclusive, in the sense that it involves the rejection of some who are not "chosen". Human choice does necessarily entail a certain exclusiveness: if I choose one or several options from among many offered I must refuse others; I cannot "choose" them all. The peculiar characteristic of God's choice, however, is that it is inclusive. In choosing "us" God does not exclude others. All men have been "chosen". The use of the term "to choose" in this context is justified by its aptness to stress the totally free initiative of God in our salvation. God has chosen us for a purpose: to be holy and blameless before him, that is with a holiness and blamelessness which is measured by his own holiness and blamelessness. We have been chosen to be like God. Moreover, this status is not the result of human endeavour (cf. v.1). We are "holy" and "blameless" only because God has chosen us to be so.

Destiny.
1:5-6.

> [5]He destined us in love to be his sons through Jesus Christ, according to the purpose of his will, [6]to the praise of his glorious grace which he freely bestowed on us in the Beloved.

All that we have said about the notion of "choice" (v.4) applies to that of "destiny" here. Paul is evidently at pains to stress the initiative of God in the work of our redemption. This is already clear in the notion of blessing (v.3) and it is also apparent in the notion of choice (v.4). But Paul leaves no doubt about it in saying that God has "destined" (lit. *pre*-destined) us. Like God's choice, his predestination is inclusive not exclusive. It is a notion which expresses God's initiative, with the added nuance of purpose or plan. In the present instance the purpose is that of sonship, which, of its very nature, is a personal relationship. Thus any idea that our "predestination" is an absolute guarantee of our status as redeemed, irrespective of our response to God's initiative, is totally excluded by this verse. If, as we have seen (cf. v.1), by "holiness" Paul does understand, first and foremost, a state of being in which we have been placed by our baptism rather than a pattern of moral behaviour, it is also true that the holiness and blamelessness mentioned in v.4 do involve our response. This remains true even though Paul would maintain that this reponse itself is the effect of God's choice and predestination. According to Paul God has chosen us *to be* holy, which means that God's antecedent sanctifying activity is also the present condition interior to our response to, or co-operation with, God's initiative. The phrase "in love" could be read either with v.4 or with v.5. In the first instance it would explain the way in which we are to be "holy and blameless", that is in love or by loving, which is a personal relationship. In this case, the holiness and blamelessness for which God has chosen man is nothing more or less than love. This would correspond perfectly to Paul's view of God as a *loving* Father (cf. v.3). If God is love, then it would seem to follow logically that to be "holy and blameless *before him*" is to love. If the phrase "in love" is read with v.5 it explains the way in which God has destined us and thus re-inforces the notion of his initiative. In any event, the reference to sonship in v.5 makes it clear beyond any doubt that the holiness to which we have been destined is the holiness of love. The father-son relationship is a relationship of love, as is the brother-brother relationship. To *be* a child of a loving father and to *be* a brother to our fellow men (v.3) means necessarily to love. Etymologically, "holy" means to be "separate" or "apart" and "blameless" means "without fault" (it is a negative notion). Defined as love, however, "holiness" becomes essentially unitive, just as "blameless-ness" becomes supremely positive.

Sonship, like blessing (v.3), choice (v.4) and pre-destina-tion was one of the prerogatives of Israel (cf. Hos 11:2). Paul recognises that "through Jesus Christ" we have become the beneficiaries of this "blessing". Thus the God whom he blesses (v.3) is not only the "Father of our Lord Jesus Christ". He is also our Father. We are the children of God neither by our natural birth nor by the Sinai covenant but only "through Jesus Christ". It is Jesus Christ who has revealed not only that God is Father but also how we are to realise our own divine sonship. He related to God as Father. If we accept him a "our Lord", that is as the supreme influence in our lives, we cannot but accept his view of God and thus recognise God as our Father.

The mediation of Christ (as Paul will recall in v.7) included his ignominious death. This probably accounts for Paul's explicit mention at this point that Christ's mediation was "according to the purpose of his will". He wishes to stress that Christ's death was not a mere accident of history or even a disaster which was rectified by the resurrection, achieved as an after-thought, like a salvaging operation. It was an integral part of God's plan for man's salvation, a plan which involved that this life should be totally human, to the point of experiencing that most human of all realities: death. And not just a death which comes to man in his bed at the end of a long and fulfilled life, but one which strikes a man brutally while he is still in his prime, a death, to boot, which is not only tragic but unjustly inflicted by other men.

It was impossible for Christ – or for any man – to "taste" death and, therefore, to share the human condition more completely than this. Such an emphasis on God's purposeful initiative with regard even to Christ's death is all the more necessary in that Christ is described as the "beloved". How could God allow Christ to suffer, if he really loved him? Paul's answer to this question is that God did not simply *allow* Christ to suffer; he *willed* him to do so. He is not concerned here to tackle the theoretical problem of Christ's suffering. His only aim is to convince his readers of God's love for them. His point is that God's love for men is so lavish that he has achieved their salvation by surrendering his "beloved" son even to the point of death. The suggestion is that God loves all other men with as great a love as (one is almost tempted to say a greater love than) he has for his own Son. It is as if he has pre-ferred all other men to his Son. It would be wrong, however, to allow ourselves at this point to be side-tracked into futile speculations on the metaphysical problem of the respective value in God's eyes of Christ and other men. All that Paul wishes to do is to show that God's love for all men is limitless. He made the same point in a similar way in his magnificent hymn to God's love in Rom 8:31-38, especially in Rom 8:32: "He who did not spare his own Son but gave him up for us all, will he not also give us all things with him?". In this passage, Paul is obviously thinking of the scene in Gen 22:12, where the angel stayed the hand of Abraham, about to slay Isaac in sacrifice, with the words: "Do not lay your hand on the lad or do anything to him; for now I know that you fear God, seeing you have not withheld your son, your only son, from me". In Eph 1:6 Paul is again very probably alluding to Gen 22, implying that just as Abraham's faith in God was measured by his willingness to abandon his only son, so God's love for men is measured by the same willingness. This connection between our verse and Gen 22 becomes even more evident from what follows later in Gen 22, when the *blessing* is linked explicitly with Abraham's willingness to sacrifice his only son: ". . . . because you have done this, and have not withheld your son, your only son, I will indeed bless you, and I will multiply your descendants as the stars of heaven and as the sand which is on the seashore. And your descendants shall possess the gate of their enemies, and by your descendants shall all the nations of the earth bless themselves, because you have obeyed my voice" (Gen 22:16-18). We have already seen references to Abraham in Eph 1:3,4 which modify considerably (if not nullify) the Jewish view of salvation history. In the present verse Paul would agree that, at the origin of salvation, there are a father and a son, but they are not Abraham and Isaac. They are God the Father and his own Son. The Abraham-Isaac relationship has stood Paul in good stead when it comes to expressing his view of salvation. According to this view, the blessing is guaranteed not because father Abraham has obeyed nor, even, because all his descendants, imitating him, have also believed, but because of God's loving grace. The unique source of salvation is God's love which is expressed finally and completely in the death of Christ. But it is Paul's Jewish education and background that has enabled him to explain this fact, by drawing on and alluding to the story of Abraham. His message is the same as that which John expresses more overtly: "For God so loved the world that he gave his only Son, that whoever believes in him should not perish but have eternal life" (Jn 3:16).

All this emphasis on what God has done for men, however, could obscure another aspect of salvation which Paul is also at pains to bring out in this verse. Just as salvation has its radical origin in God, so it has as its ultimate end not men but God himself or, as Paul puts it here: "the praise of his glorious grace". God has saved men, that is made them complete human beings, in order that they may praise him or, more precisely, for the "glory of his grace". We have already considered what God's "grace" is for Paul. It is God's love for us which, because it is totally unmerited, is his favour toward us. "Glory" here means manifestation or revelation. It is in the "beloved" that God has revealed himself as the "lover". "Glorious grace" is revealed grace. Mystic that he is, Paul sees in Christ the complete manifestation of God's favour towards men. On this point too he and John are united: "And the Word became flesh and dwelt among us, full of grace and truth; we have beheld his glory, glory as of the only Son from the Father" (Jn 1:14). To recognise Christ as Son is to recognise God as Father; to accept Christ as the beloved is to accept God as the lover, as the one who, of his very nature, is favourable. Such a recognition or acceptance takes place in faith, but it is expressed in praise. This praise, for Paul, is nothing more or less than the explicit and expressed recognition of God, as he has revealed himself in his saving work. It is men's ultimate response to God's gift; it is the articulation, the orchestration of faith. It is praise of God himself, as he is in himself, that is as Father, as love. The heart of the Christian revelation is not that God is Creator, Lord, Omnipotent *and* Father, but that he *is* Father, *is* love.

It is evident, therefore, that there is no opposition between man's salvation and the praise of God. Since this praise is the expressed acknowledgement of God's love, which, of its very nature, is directed towards men, it is the consummation of salvation itself. It is the full participation, by mind, heart and body, in this salvation. It is the "Amen" to God's saving work. True Christian praise is addressed to God not simply as Creator, etc. but as Father. The archetype of this praise is, in fact, the "Our Father", the prayer which Paul himself evokes in this praise or blessing in which he is presently engaged. Although Paul himself is here voicing an actual blessing, the praise of which he reminds his readers is not merely a question of the tongue. It is, first and foremost, an attitude of being. It is the praise which is given to God by the very fact that we *are* "holy and blameless" (v.4), that we *are* God's sons (v.5). According to Paul, praise or worship is not just a part – however an important a part – of the Christian's life, such as might be confined to special times and places. It is the whole of life considered as renewed by God through Christ. It is essentially a *living* praise or worship. The Christian worships God by leading a life which corresponds to God's revelation. But this revelation is essentially for men's good, being the manifestation of God as love. Thus there is no conflict between men's good and God's glory. In fact, for Paul the two are identically the same. God's glory is men's salvation in the fullest sense of their participation in God's holiness and their becoming his children. Such worship of God is less a giving to him than a receiving from him. The God whom the Christians worship is Father, and as such his will is not to receive anything from men (after all, what *can* men give to God?), except the acknowledgement that he is Father. As Irenaeus will put it later: "Living man is the glory of God".

Redemption.
1:7-8.

> [7]In him we have redemption through his blood, the forgiveness of our trespasses, according to the riches of his grace [8]which he lavished upon us.

So far in this blessing Paul has concentrated on God's plan for "us". He has, as it were, contemplated salvation from God's side. But now, with the "we have", he turns to our side of salvation, to what it means for us here and now. The two main ideas which he announces in v.7 are redemption and forgiveness. These ideas, like those which we have already encountered in the blessing: blessing, choice, holiness, sonship, were very familiar to the Jews of Paul's time and, indeed, they are comprehensible only when seen against the background of Judaism. They are metaphors, drawn from the Old Testament and other Jewish literature, used to explain the meaning of the Christ-event – in the most immediate context, the significance of Christian baptism. Paul is here trying to explain the baptismal experience.

If the themes of blessing, choice and destiny are, as we have seen, particularly associated, in the biblical tradition, with the book of Genesis and the person of Abraham, it is now to the book of Exodus and the person of Moses that we must look if we are to begin to grasp the meaning of Paul's expressions in v.7. The escape of the Hebrew slaves from Egypt, under Moses' leadership, as this is presented in the book of Exodus, was considered by the Jews as *the* great act of *redemption* on God's part in favour of his people. Moreover, this redemption or liberation is closely associated with *blood*, that is the blood of the paschal lamb (Ex 12:22-23). In a sense, it was "through" the blood of the paschal lamb that the Israelites were redeemed. Such "redemption" is a metaphor, evoking both the practice of achieving the manumission of a slave and the custom of "buying back" a child who had been offered previously to the deity. This symbolism may be lost on us today, but it exercised a very powerful influence on Paul's contemporaries. Already, in Old Testament times, the Exodus "redemption" was considered as a model for the new, spiritual redemption of the return from the Babylonian Exile. In the first redemption, Moses, the mediator of the Exodus, had merely ordered his people to sprinkle the blood of the lamb on their doorposts. In the new redemption, envisaged by the anonymous prophet of the Exile who penned Is 40-55, the mediator of the new Exodus would spill his own blood (Is 52:13-53:12). Paul's Jewish contemporaries also saw an expiatory value in the blood of the paschal lamb. Thus what Paul is saying here becomes very clear: for him Christ is both the true paschal lamb and the true Servant prophesied in Is 52:13-53:12. The redemption announced in the Exodus and the return from Exile is realised fully in him. The very real blood which Christ shed on the cross is the clue which Paul takes up to understand the profound meaning of this death. It enables him to interpret and explain Christ's death in terms of the Jewish cult.

The mention of the "forgiveness of our trespasses" conveys basically the same message. Not only did "trespasses" become possible with the advent of the Mosaic law (Rom 4:15), but the same law, given at the time of the Exodus, contains elaborate provisions for the "forgiveness" of these trespasses. This forgiveness is connected with the blood of sacrifices, especially with the blood of the expiation sacrifice, offered once a year on the Day of Expiations in accordance with the ritual laid down in Lev 16. Thus both trespasses and their forgiveness pre-suppose the Mosaic law. Paul is here expressing his conviction that Christ's death, appropriated by each Christian at his baptism, achieves all that is envisaged by the sacrificial system of the Mosaic law.

Terms like "redemption" and "trespasses" have become so much a part of the private language of religious people that their essential link with a particular world-view is often overlooked. In fact, such terms have no meaning outside the religious settings in which they originated and were developed. Modern man should acknowledge frankly that this religious language is not verifiable today, simply because the religious background it supposes no longer exists. Certainly Paul is not to be blamed for this predicament. In the present context, at least, he is only praying out loud and expressing his *own* experience (albeit in the conviction that his experience will have some relevance to "us", that is his contemporaries).

Now it is no exaggeration to say that Paul, as a Jew, was obsessed with the twin ideas of redemption from sin and forgiveness of trespasses. For him these were not "religious" ideas, divorced from the affairs of his everyday life. They were vital issues. It was natural, therefore, that in his conversion experience he should realise that everything that he had striven for and expected within his religion of Judaism – in the present instance, redemption and forgiveness – had been achieved for him in Christ. In other words, redemption and forgiveness represented two aspects of the fulfilment of all his hopes and aspirations which Paul, as a Jew, experienced as being achieved in Christ. If we – the readers of the twentieth century – are to make Paul's experience our own, we must somehow be able to pass beyond the metaphors in question and arrive at the reality – which is just as real for us as it was for Paul – which these metaphors are attempting to express. This reality seems to be in the area of our "hopes and aspirations". We need to ask ourselves what, within these "hopes and aspirations", is our equivalent to Paul's "redemption" and "forgiveness". Paul's profound experience becomes ours too, once we realise that everything for which we strive and hope, at the very depths of our being, has been given to us in Christ.

The mention of Christ's blood could give rise to the wrong impression that the redemption and forgiveness which Paul has in mind were in some way earned or merited by Christ. It might even appear that Christ's blood was some kind of "price" paid for the redemption and forgiveness. Paul clearly precludes such interpretations by insisting that they, too, are the fruits of God's grace. Both the redemption and the forgiveness are pure gifts. The reference to grace in this context reinforces what we have already gathered from v.5: Christ's death represents the summit of the Father's love for men.

Revelation.
1:9-10.

> [9]For he has made known to us in all wisdom and insight the mystery of his will, according to his purpose which he set forth in Christ [10]as a plan for the fullness of time, to unite all things in him, things in heaven and things on earth.

At the end of this first part of his *berakah* Paul arrives at what is undoubtedly his most important motive and the one which has been supposed throughout his prayer so far: the actual revelation of God's saving plan. Without the knowledge of this plan, communicated by God himself, the prayer of blessing would obviously be impossible. Indeed, salvation itself would be impossible, in so far as it requires a conscious, informed and explicit acceptance on men's part.

Thus, according to Paul, not only is the Christ-event the full revelation of God's saving love. If it is to be known, it has to be revealed by God himself. It is God who had made it known. This is one of the points on which Paul is most insistent throughout his letters. He puts it most poignantly perhaps in Gal 1:15-16: "But when he who had set me apart before I was born, and had called me through his grace, was pleased to reveal his Son to me, in order that I might preach him among the Gentiles, I did not confer with flesh and blood". But the idea that the Christ-event is revealed is central to his theology. He loses no opportunity to remind his readers that the Christian "mystery" is attained not by mere human effort, however strenuous or intelligent, but only by God's loving initiative. Faith (v.1) is men's loving acceptance of this initiative. The Christian religion is revelation in both content and form.

We have already considered how the modern man wishing to make sense of Paul's experience must learn to understand the terms in which this experience is expressed and refine his own ideas accordingly (v.7). It is no less important to consider the implications of the fact that the Christian religion is essentially a revealed religion. It implies, for instance, that for men living in our pluralist, multi-cultural, technological society the claims of Christianity cannot be proven, any more than its tenets can be assumed, let alone imposed by any external authorities. Access to the Christian religion, for each and every individual, is no different in the twentieth century from what it was in the first. It is possible only by faith, which is God's personal gift to every believer. At this point it is perhaps worthwhile recalling the baptismal background of Ephesians. Paul is here voicing the sort of prayer which may have often been uttered on the occasion of baptism, just after the neophyte had "risen" from the font. He is reminding his readers that it is at their baptism – the "seal" of their faith – that they have received the full revelation of the "mystery" of God's will. Only the person who believes and who has been baptised can appreciate what Paul is saying here.

Paul here refers to the Christ-event as a "mystery". In itself, this terms means "secret", but in the Bible it means the "secret *which has been revealed*". God's saving plan is a "mystery" in the sense that it is not accessible to the unaided human intelligence. But it is not a "secret" in so far as it is disclosed by God. Ironically – once account is taken of revelation and faith – there are no real "mysteries" or "secrets" for the Christian. In Christ God has revealed both himself and his saving plan fully, even though men have not yet fully understood this "mystery". Such an understanding, beginning with faith and baptism, is a gradual and continuing process, co-terminous with human existence itself.

The fact that Paul insists on the revelatory character of the Christ-event, even calling it a "mystery" inaccessible to bare human reason, does not mean, however, that it is irrational or in some way competes with human intelligence. In fact, he states clearly that God has made the mystery known "in all wisdom and insight". This phrase could refer to the way in which God has revealed the mystery, but it could just as well describe the way we now know it. Although God's saving plan could not be known by merely human wisdom and insight, once it is revealed and accepted by faith it becomes "all wisdom and insight". It is the perfection of human wisdom and understanding. The believer, in believing, does not renounce his intelligence. Rather, he allows it to be developed and perfected. The only condition is that he does not try, as did the men of Babel (Gen 11:1-9) to pull himself up "by his own boot laces". Paul expresses the same idea in 1 Cor 2:6: "Yet among the mature we do impart wisdom, although it is not a wisdom of this age or of the rulers of this age, who are doomed to pass away. But we impart a secret and hidden wisdom of God, which God declared before the ages for our glorification".

What Paul says about the knowledge of salvation must also apply to salvation itself. Although this is a pure gift of God, unattainable by man himself, it is still needed by man. According to Paul, a man who is not saved, in the sense of accepting the "good news" represented by Christ, is not a whole man, is not "mature" (1 Cor 2:6).

If we have been given knowledge of the "mystery" "in all knowledge and insight", it follows that our faith is not blind. True Christian faith is informed faith, just as mature human intelligence is faith-inspired. We cannot learn God's transcendant word without the medium of our own human language, any more than we understand the ultimate mystery of our existence without the revelation of God. To this extent, theology or "God-talk" is not the private reserve of a few privileged academics. Thinking and talking about God and his saving plan are the responsibility of every Christian. They are necessary ingredients of prayer itself – as Paul's own prayer here illustrates.

Paul has already expressed his convictions that the Christ-event was not an accident of human history but the result of a real "purpose" on God's part (v.5). He repeats the idea here (v.9) and calls this purpose explicitly a "plan" (v.10). This plan includes not only what we have already seen as having taken place in the past: blessing, choice, destiny, redemption and revelation, but also what will happen in "the fulness of time". Paul obviously considered that the Christ-event had inaugurated this "fulness of time" (Gal 4:4). But it is just as evident that the Christ-event itself is not yet fully accomplished. The essence of God's plan, centred on Christ, is expressed in a Greek term meaning to "resume", "sum-up" or, literally, "re-capitulate". Paul here sees God's plan as one for the "resumption", the "summing up", the "re-capitulation" of all things in Christ. The notion implies two main ideas: renewal and headship.

Renewal itself suggests that previously all things were disunited and lacking in consistency. There could be here yet another illusion to the tower of Babel story, the point being that the harmony among men which was disrupted by the "original sin" of Babel has now been restored by God in Christ. Precisely *how* Christ is to be seen as the "head" of all creation, Paul does not say here. The answer to this question probably has something to do with the "wisdom and insight" which Paul has just mentioned. It is only by meditation and profound contemplation that we will be able to share the fruits of Paul's own experience, which here can only be described as "mystical". Remember, Paul is at prayer.

It is well worth noting that Paul speaks not about the re-capitulation of all *men* in Christ but, rather, about the re-capitulation of all *things*. The explicit reference to things "in heaven", apart from re-inforcing the idea of universality, is probably an echo of Paul's controversy with the Colossian Gnostics for whom Christ was nothing more than one of the beings who inhabited the "heavens". In Colossians, writing in a more polemic mood, Paul was at pains to stress that Christ was far superior to anything in the heavens: "for in him all things were created, in heaven and on earth, visible and invisible, whether thrones or dominions or principalities or authorities – all things were created through him and for him" (Col 1:16). This connection with Colossians possibly provides part of the answer to the question raised earlier about the meaning of Paul's expression: "to re-capitulate all things in Christ". Against the background of the ancient cosmology, according to which the universe was composed of four basic layers: the underworld, the earth, the air and the heavens, Paul expresses his conviction that, since Christ (who lived on *earth*) died (that is descended into the *underworld*), was raised from the dead and ascended into the heavens (by passing through the *air*), he has exercised his influence in all these spheres and, being now at God's right hand, has had all things "placed under his feet". In this sense he is "head" of everything. He has cosmic supremacy. But this is only a part of the answer to our question. In Colossians it is a question of the *creation* of the universe in Christ. Here it is a question of the "re-capitulation" of the universe in Christ, with the suggestion of a previous disharmony subsequent to an original harmony. It could be that Paul is here thinking beyond Babel to that other "original sin" described in Gen 3. It is by this sin that the pristine harmony of man with his environment was disrupted and that the material creation itself was infected and put in need of redemption. Paul himself has already argued to this effect in Romans: "For the creation waits with eager longing for the revealing of the sons of God; for the creation was subjected to futility, not of its own will but by the will of him who subjected it in hope; because the creation itself will be set free from its bondage to decay and obtain the glorious liberty of the children of God" (Rom 8:19-21). Thus for Paul salvation concerns not only men – let alone just men's souls – but the whole of creation, men's whole environment.

Naturally modern man does not hold to the ancient cosmology, any more than he subscribes to the biblical view of human diversity or the apparent lack of harmony in the universe. But, for all this, he need not be a victim of the "baby and the bathwater" syndrome. We must "de-mythologise" Paul's thought, even if this means that we then have to "re-mythologise" it in view of our own conceptions of the universe. For those who share Paul's faith experience, his message has a perennial value, despite the ephemeral language in which it is expressed.

In the present instance, Paul is evincing his conviction that Christ is the God-given key to the understanding of the mystery of existence. He is the supreme value in relation to which everything else is to be measured. In view of Christ, who died and is now alive, the universe is not marked down for destruction. It is designed if not to "last" certainly to be re-newed.

It is striking that Paul ends this first part of his *berakah* where he began: in heaven (vv.3,10). Christ is actually "in heaven", in the sense that he has passed personally through life and resurrection. All believers are "in heaven", in so far as they are united with Christ by faith and baptism. Our final destiny, as God's children, is to be actually with Christ "in heaven". Thus our present state is not definitive. To the extent that we believe, however, we already share in Christ's supremacy over the rest of creation. We are, as it were, stretched between two dimensions: that of earth and that of "heaven". It is this fact that forms the basis of the Christians' enterprise and mission: to be instruments in the "re-capitulation" of the universe in Christ. As Paul will insist later in this letter, the Christians' final destiny in "heaven", far from being an excuse to avoid involvement in the "world", is in fact a spur to this involvement. As we have seen, "heaven" is a way of speaking about the boundlessness of Christ's saving power. Inspired by faith in Christ, Christians are able to be the channels of this power, albeit only in their own limited sphere.

THE UNION OF JEWS AND GENTILES.
1:11-14.

Paul has just made it very clear that for him salvation is essentially cosmic, that is, it concerns the whole universe and not only human beings. His own main concern at present, however, is with the men he is addressing in his letter. In what may appear to us to be a very facile and simplistic way, Paul sees his readers as belonging to one of two categories, according to their birth: the Jews or the Gentiles. And the first effect of the "re-capitulation" of all things in Christ is, precisely, the re-unificaton of humanity, divided into these two parts, into one community with Christ as its "head". This insight of a planned united mankind is the answer to the problem which had so vexed Paul in Rom 8-11 (v.4). It is as if Paul's imprisonment has been the heaven-sent opportunity to put the relationship between the Jews and the Gentiles in a new perspective. Previously he had viewed salvation historically, beginning with Abraham or even with Adam and ending with Christ. Now he views it as a mystery, that is as the revelation of a plan which transcends time and space and of which the history of Israel is only a part.

The Jews.
1:11-12.

> ¹¹In him, according to the purpose of him who accomplishes all things according to the counsel of his will, ¹²we who first hoped in Christ have been destined and appointed to live for the praise of his glory.

For Paul the only real difference between the Jews who have accepted Christ and Gentile Christians is that the former previously hoped in Christ. This prior history was all part of God's plan, according to which it is only in Christ that the Jews fully realise their vocation to glorify God (v.6). The Jewish religion's only *raison d'être* is to prepare the way for Christ. It is he alone who gives consistency to Jewish hopes and aspirations – a truth to which Paul, as a Jew himself, is well able to testify.

But it is not only *Jewish* Christians who have been destined and appointed to live (or, literally, to *exist*) for the praise of God's glory. This applies to all men (v.6).

The Gentiles.
1:13-14.

> ¹³In him you also, who have heard the word of truth, the gospel of your salvation, and have believed in him, were sealed with the promised Holy Spirit, ¹⁴which is the guarantee of our inheritance until we acquire possession of it, to the praise of his glory.

If the characteristic of Jewish Christians is that they previously hoped in Christ, that of Gentile Christians is that they have believed in Christ by hearing the gospel. It is obvious that the Jewish Christians also had to do this. But Paul's point is that hearing and believing were the Gentile Christians' *only* access to Christ, whereas the Jews had the prior witness of their own religion. Final access to salvation for all men is possible only through faith by means of hearing (Rom 10:17). Salvation comes to them in a "word" which has to be heard and in "good news" which has to be believed. As we have already seen (v.8), God's revelation brings "all wisdom and insight", but this revelation is not attained by any kind of "vision", be this physical or spiritual (1 Cor 1:22). It is received by hearing and believing. Without a doubt Paul is here evoking the apostolic preaching and the commitment of faith given to this preaching. Baptism is the visible expression, the "seal" of this faith and, as such, it is the moment when we receive the very "substance" of salvation, that is the Holy Spirit, the "spiritual blessing" (v.3) which was promised to the Jews but is received by all men – Jews included – by faith. It is because this Spirit is "Holy", that is, the Spirit of holiness, that we, upon receiving it, become holy (v.4), just as we become God's sons by having the Spirit of his Son (v.5; Gal 4:6; Rom 8:15). It is by God's Spirit that we participate in the reality of God. It is evident that Christians of Jewish origin were not exempted from this "sealing" or baptism, any more than they were exempted from faith (Acts 2:37-41). As this passage in the Acts shows very clearly, it is in baptism that the Jews, too, receive the promised Holy Spirit. Thus the last part of v.13 refers both to Jewish and to Gentile Christians, who are now united in one community, in virtue of their common existence in Christ, mediated by faith and expressed by the "seal" of the Holy Spirit. The "seal" is evidently an external sign – baptism – but the Holy Spirit is an inner experience, verifiable only by those who share it. This Spirit, like the Father (vv.2,3) and the Beloved (Son) (v.6), is a metaphor used to express the experienced reality of the relationship established with God by baptism. It is then that we become sons of God the Father

in Christ the Son *through* the Spirit. Of the three metaphors: Father, Son and Spirit, the first two are fairly easy
to understand, since we all have some knowledge, if only
indirect, of fathers and sons. But "spirit" is the vaguest of
notions. In the Bible the Spirit of God, the Spirit, the Holy
Spirit is God himself, considered as active, powerful, the
source of life. It is a term which thus expresses the communicability of God. To receive the Spirit of God means to be
enlivened by God himself. To have the Spirit of the Son
means to be a son. The fact that the term "spirit" (which
describes man's specific nature) should be used to denote
this God-ward relationship is by no means coincidental.
In fact, the Christian has the Spirit of God only if, and in so
far as, his spirit is of God. He has the Holy Spirit only if he
is really holy in his spirit. At the same time, it is true to say
that a man can be holy only through the Holy Spirit.

Later Christian theology will interpret these three
metaphors as a "Trinity" of persons and will even attempt
to contemplate the inner life of God on this basis. But Paul
himself does not go this far. As we have seen (v.6), Paul is
concerned not with God as he is "in himself" but as he has
revealed himself to men. His intention is to describe not the
interior life of God but the plan of man's salvation.

In the present context, therefore, the Holy Spirit is the
new experienced relationship of holiness and divine sonship. This experience is the first instalment or the guarantee
of the inheritance which will be acquired only at the end of
time. We meet here again the tension between the "already"
and the "not yet" which we saw in v.10. On the one hand,
with the arrival of Christ the "fulness of time" has already
come; we are already in the "last days" (Acts 2:17). On the
other hand, God's saving plan has not yet been finally
accomplished, since the universe is not yet submitted
totally to Christ. Thus if we are stretched spatially between
heaven and earth (v.10) we are also torn temporally between
the present and the future. We have already become heirs
of the promise made to Abraham (v.3), but we will receive
full possession of this inheritance only at the end of time.

This possession will mark the completion of our redemption, which will also serve as a revelation of God's "glory". The Father will be fully revealed as Father when his children receive their inheritance.

EXCURSUS:
Father, Son, Holy Spirit,
The Trinity.

IN THIS INITIAL PRAYER (1:3-14) of the first part (1:3-3:21), a Christian prayer that takes much for granted, there is reference to the Father, the Lord Jesus Christ and the Holy Spirit. It is surely worth our while to pause and study Paul's thought more closely. Father, Son and Spirit must mightily concern the Christian.

Father

Paul is a theologian, in the strict sense of this term, that is he is a man who talks reflectively about *theos* or God.

It is vital for an understanding of his thought to realise that, despite his involvement with his fellow men and his deep pastoral concern for their salvation, he is, first and foremost, "a man of God", that is his primary preoccupation is the God whom he serves. Indeed, in view of what we are going to see about his understanding of this God, we ought rather to say that it is precisely because he is a man of *this* God that he is so committed to the service of his fellows. In his apostolate Paul exemplifies his own principle that the whole law – including the command to love God – is accomplished in the service of one's neighbour (Gal 5:14).

Paul's conversion experience did not entail a change of God. The God whom he worships as a "slave of Christ" is still the God to whom he was introduced as a child and whom he served wholeheartedly as a Pharisee. Only this experience involved a further, deeper understanding of this God, one which completed the revelation which is found already in the Old Testament. This God is unique, creator of the universe, omnipotent and, most strikingly, personal and personally concerned about his creation, particularly about mankind. It is especially with regard to this personal character of God that Paul's understanding has developed. He sees in Christ both an unheard-of intensity and an unimaginable extension of God's involvement with and concern for creation. For *this* man Jesus is understood as God's "son" in a totally new sense from that in which, for example, the people of Israel was God's "son". He is God's unique Son, but not in an exclusive sense. This uniqueness itself is communicable to all other men who are destined to be "sons" – in this new "unique" sense – *in* Christ. Thus the privilege of divine sonship, concentrated in Christ, is extendable to all other men. In other words, in Christ, Paul has come to a new understanding of his God as Father.

In Ephesians, as elsewhere, Paul stresses that he has arrived at this new understanding of God through the revelation of God himself. God is a person who reveals, who communicates. And this simple fact – one which is often overlooked or taken for granted – is of prime importance for an understanding of the Christian religion. In itself, this fact implies the essence of the Christian religion itself, namely the desire of God – the omnipotent and omniscient creator, the "ground of being" – to communicate, that is to become "one" with his creation, to enable this creation to participate in his life. This – in a nutshell – is what we will see to be God's "plan". But, for the moment, let us just note that without revelation, that is God himself telling us, we would not know about this plan. Thus this revelation is itself a "grace", perhaps the greatest of God's gifts. It is certainly the most fundamental, in the sense that, without it, all the others would be futile in that they would not be "known".

Revelation, therefore, implies a great deal about God himself. It shows that, although he is "God", that is the omnipotent creator, he is not a "loner", one who wants to be alone. He wants to be with others, even his creatures, and he wants them to be with him. In understanding God fundamentally as "Revealer", Paul does indeed meet God as he is "in himself". But this "self" of God is in no way isolated from his creation. Such an idea of "self", of "person" – as that which exists apart, alone, unrelated with others – would be totally alien to Paul. His God is a person who speaks, relates, communicates, shares, is – quite literally – "outward moving", "extrovert". All that Paul knows and says about his God concerns God's relationship with his creation. He knows no other God than the God of love.

If revelation is the fundamental relationship between men and God, what is the object of this revelation? According to Paul, God *in* Christ has revealed his grace, his power, his wisdom and his glory.

In Christ God has manifested his grace, that is his favour, solicitude, love for all men. This grace is implied in the fact of revelation itself, in so far as God, of his own free initiative, has willed to relate with his creatures. But in Ephesians Paul, by repeated mention of the term "grace", emphasizes that our relationship with God is one of pure gift. The Christ-event itself is the expression of grace (1:6; 2:7). More particularly, it is by grace that we have redemption and the forgiveness of sins (1:7; 2:8), that we are saved (2:8). Paul's apostolate is a grace (3:1,7,8), and the church is constructed by grace (4:7,11). This insistence on grace obviously safeguards God's purely free initiative with which he intervenes for man's salvation. It is, after all, necessary for Paul to stress this freedom, in that he presents God as one who, of his very nature, communicates with his creation. Paul holds that this communication, on God's part, as vital and essential as it is, is nevertheless not necessary but free. Man has no right to it; God is perfectly free in initiating it. It is the effect of his purely gratuitous love.

God's grace is revealed, above all, by the fact that the relationship established between men and God by the Christ-event is *par excellence* a loving relationship, that is divine sonship (1:5). God's grace, favour or love towards men could not be conveyed more tellingly than by his expressed intention to make them his beloved sons.

To want to save man, however, is one thing; to be *able* to do so is quite another. Thus Paul emphasizes not only that God is gracious towards man, but also that he is well able to accomplish his loving design. Paul does this by spotlighting the revelation of God's power in the Christ-event. This power is essentially *saving* power, that is the ability to overcome all the forces inimical to man and to bring him to his final destiny as God's son. According to Paul, God has displayed this power pre-eminently in the resurrection and exaltation of Christ (1:19-23) which, being God's grace towards us, is the model of our own triumph over death and every other evil force (2:1-10). But it is also the power which is, or should be, presently at work in us (1:19; 3:16,18,20) and which, with grace, is the source of the apostolate (3:7). God's power is what enables us to achieve his grace; but it is also a grace, precisely because it is *his* power and not *ours*, even though it is at work within us. The fact that we can arrive at our final destiny only by God's power, itself implies that this destiny is a grace.

The Christ-event is also an expression of God's wisdom. Like God's grace and his power, this wisdom, centred as it is in Christ (that is, the crucified Jesus), is paradoxical. Only by revelation can the Jesus story become the Christ-event and thus be seen as "wisdom" (1:9,17; 3:10), that is a sensible enterprise. Wisdom in the Bible is a supremely practical attribute. The "wise" man is the one who knows how to succeed. God's wisdom is his way of achieving success for his creation. This way is precisely at the antipodes of man's (cf. Is 55:8-9), as is abundantly clear from the cross (viewed without the light of the resurrection). But it is in fact this way that leads man to his final destiny, being the manner in which God exercises his power (2:1-10). Also like God's grace and power, his wisdom is a function of his extraversion, that is it is in favour of his creation.

Clearly connected with God's wisdom is his design or plan for man's salvation. Paul calls this a "mystery" (1:9; 2:3,9). According to him, man's salvation is not the result of God's intervention subsequent to a "fall" on man's part which annulled or jeopardized an original plan. This salvation is part of God's original plan for his creation. His plan "from eternity" is "salvific"; and this plan is the expression of his wisdom. It has two aspects: first, the granting of the status of divine sonship on all men through Christ (1:5); second, the recapitulation of the universe in Christ. The historical Jesus or, more precisely, the Christ-event, is the focal point of this plan in time and space. But the plan itself is eternal, that is it was made before the creation of the world (1:4). This "eternal" character of God's plan again suggests his sovereign freedom with regard to his creation. In making this plan he could not be determined by anything other than his own love for his creatures.

Finally, Paul sees the Christ-event as being charged with God's glory (1:6,17,18; 3:16,21). In the Bible, God's glory is the very nature or essence of God, in so far as this is able to be manifested and communicated. Paul claims that in Christ God has manifested and communicated himself to men. This means that his grace is "glorious" (1:6), that he is the "Father of glory" (1:17). Both manifestation and communication, however, are two-sided. For there to be true manifestation some recognition must take place. Similarly, true communication requires acceptance or reception. Thus for there to be true glory, even God's glory, creation must recognise and accept God as he has revealed himself. The ultimate end of God's revelation is his glory, but this glory is not external to the revelation. It is precisely by acknowledging God as Father and receiving him as such that man allow God's glory to be realized. For his glory is nothing more or less than his nature which is love. God is "glorified" or praised by his creatures when he is recognized effectively as love.

The Lord Jesus Christ

God the Father's gracious, loving plan for his creation is two-fold: to make all men his children and to establish unity and harmony among all things. The message of Ephesians is that he accomplishes this plan through and in Jesus Christ. He is the revelation of this plan in person, the "incarnation" of the Father's grace or love. Paul's theme is very simple: if you want to know God's plan for the universe and for man in particular, that is if you want to know the meaning of reality, just contemplate Jesus Christ. "Contemplate" is the key word here. This contemplation implies and requires faith, that is the recognition and the acceptance of God's revelation. It also requires that empathy with the content of the revelation which we will see to be love. Without the commitment of faith and love Jesus Christ is meaningless.

In fact the Jesus whom Paul himself is continually contemplating throughout Ephesians is not just the man who lived and preached in Palestine, ending his life on a cross. He certainly is *this man*, and if we allow what Paul says about him to detract from or obscure the fact that Jesus is totally and completely human, we will not even begin to understand Paul's view of salvation. Paul's gospel depends upon Jesus' humanity. If Jesus were not human, that is one of us, he just would not be the final and definitive "good news" that Paul claims him to be. The "good news" of Jesus is that God wants and is able to do for all others *precisely* what he has done for Jesus, that he wants all others *to be* precisely who Jesus is for him. Everything that God has revealed Jesus to be, including (indeed especially) his unique filial relationship, is communicable. If it were not communicable, it would not have been revealed. If the revealed Jesus were to have something or to be someone totally alien to us he would not be "good news" for us. Thus it is vital that Jesus is human and that everything verifiable of him has a reference to all other men and women.

Nevertheless, in Ephesians (as indeed generally elsewhere is his letters) Paul does not view Jesus from the angle of his earthly life, that is from the standpoint of our present existence. He considers his total revealed existence which includes his full participation in our present condition but also transcends it and embraces full participation in God's life as God's son. Here it is important to refer to the point made in the last paragraph and to stress that the existence of Jesus which we are discussing is not a "divine" existence distinct from a "human" one. It is his *human* existence which is given a new, "divine" dimension by God the Father at this resurrection and exaltation. Being revealed to men, this new dimension of human existence becomes "good news" for them. It means that they are destined to be "like" Jesus, other sons of God, to share fully in God's life and, in so doing, to achieve *human* fulfilment. Jesus' resurrection and exaltation prove (to the eyes of faith,

that is) that, far from there being any insuperable obstacles
to this destiny, it is precisely by overcoming all opposition,
including and especially death, that this destiny is attained.
It is this view of Jesus that makes him "good news".

Just as Paul considers even God himself in his relationship to his creatures, so he sees Jesus only with regard to
other men. For Paul Jesus is "Christ" and "Lord". Although
the term "Christ" is already part of a proper name and has,
therefore, lost most of its immediate references to the
Messiah, it still retains some of the undertones of its original
meaning and conveys the idea that Jesus (this name means
"Saviour") has a messianic role to play in God's plan *for*
his creation. The term "Lord", while ascribing to Jesus the
title reserved for God in the Old Testament, expresses more
immediately Paul's (and, therefore, his communities')
recognition of Jesus' sovereignty and supreme influence.
In accepting Jesus as "Lord" men necessarily allow him to
be the most important factor in their lives, they take him
as their model and exemplar, the one whom they follow.
Thus Jesus' name (like that of God: Father) describes
Jesus not as he is "in himself" but what he is for other
men. If Paul's God is a "God for others", his Jesus is a "man
for others". If God is love, Jesus is the revelation of this love.

But how, precisely, is Jesus the revelation of God's love?
In attempting to answer this question, we have to bear
constantly in mind that revelation is two-sided: it requires
a revealer and one who receives the revelation. If there is
no reception of what is revealed, then – strictly speaking –
there is no revelation. In Ephesians Paul considers the
revelation of God's love in Christ from two points of view:
first, from the point of view of his death; second, from the
point of view of his resurrection. Significantly, where it is a
question of the death Paul speaks of Christ's own activity,
while when it is a question of his resurrection he speaks of
God's action upon Jesus. It is as if the dying Jesus is more
the model or exemplar of how we should behave, while
the raised and elevated Christ is more the example of what
God has in store for all men.

In speaking of Christ's death Paul stresses particularly its reconciling and peace-making role (2:14-16). It is Christ himself who, by dying on the cross, has both destroyed enmity between men and reconciled men with God. These are really two sides of the same coin. Because, for Paul, God is love; the essence of sin, that is everything that is contrary to God, is hatred, the opposite of love. By dying in the way that he did, that is out of loving obedience to his Father, not cursing his executioners but forgiving them and praying for them, *this man Jesus* introduced a new dimension into human existence. He revealed a new spiritual universe in which all men could live: the universe of love, in which a person acts no longer for himself but for others, in imitation of, and by participating in the life of, God who, as Father, *exists* for his creation. By his self-sacrificing death (5:2) Jesus revealed that it is possible for a man to love, literally, to the "end", ultimately and completely, without self-interest or reserve. In his way Jesus reveals not only God's "objective" love for men, in so far as he is the "beloved" surrendered by the Father (1:6). He also reveals God's love "subjectively", that is he freely enters into the Father's loving design for his universe. He reveals *man* lovingly involved in this plan and shows precisely how our destiny on this earth is fulfilled: by self-giving love. But he does this precisely as part of God's objective revelation, as part of the Father's plan. If he were the only man to have loved like God, this plan would not be a success. Jesus is essentially the "man *for* others".

Since Jesus reveals God's love, in the biblical sense of revelation (that is, communication), he not only shows that it *is* possible to love like God. He also *makes* it possible for other men to love in this way. In this regard, it is important to remember that Paul is contemplating Christ through the prism of Christian experience. He can speak about Christ as the revelation of God's love only because he knows that this revelation has in fact been received, that men, precisely through their faith in Christ, have succeeded in loving others to the point of giving themselves completely in death. Paul knows that "Christ works" in a way that was impossible, for instance, for the Jewish law. According to Paul, Christ, considered as revelation, is God's infallibly efficacious "word" incarnate (cf. Is 55:10-11). It produces what it signifies. All that is required is that it should be heard.

Given the fact that sin is fundamentally the refusal to love, it is easy to see how Christ's death, being the effective revelation of love, brings about the "remission" of sins. Sin and love are incompatible. In the universe of love inaugurated by Christ there is no room for hatred, enmity, strife and contention – for anything, in fact, which destroys or which does not contribute towards the unity between men and the harmony in the universe which is God's plan for his creation. Being right with God necessarily involves being at peace with his creation.

When it comes to Christ's resurrection, Paul insists more on what God has done for other men in and through Christ (1:20-2:10). This action is a revelation of the Father's love, is so far as it is offered to men as an example or model of what he has in mind for them. This resurrection is not presented as any kind of return to life. It is the introduction into a new kind of existence, which transcends our present condition. In the case of the individual Jesus, it clearly involves the victory over physical death and the enjoyment of a life which is completely beyond our understanding. But, significantly, Paul does not concentrate either on what the resurrection meant for Jesus himself or on what we might call its "futuristic" aspect, that is how it concerns our physical death. Paul's unique concern is with those who are now alive. He wishes to convince them of God's love for them in the here and now. He is not interested in instructing them about the "after life". Thus Christ's resurrection is presented as a paradigm, the "spiritual" resurrection of the baptised. Just as Christ's death, considered as a revelation of love, really signifies a death to sin, so his resurrection signifies the new life of love, the freedom from selfishness, the immunity from all alien forces. Christ's resurrection is a proof of God's love for us because it shows that he wants man to live. Here again Paul is viewing the resurrection through the prism of Christian experience. He knows the experience of those who have died and lived in baptism. He is thus able to present the dying and resurrection of Christ as a telling expression of this experience.

But Christ's resurrection is a revelation of God's love in another sense. As the counterpart to his death, it represents the positive, fulfilling aspect of self-giving love. It is precisely through his death that Christ enters into his resurrection. Thus the resurrection is a revelation of the ultimate achievement that is possible only through self-less giving. It is a proof that loving is a worthwhile activity.

The Holy Spirit

It is God the Father who is the principal cause of our salvation. He conceives his plan to make all men his children and to unify the universe "before the foundation of the world" (1:4) and he executes it in "the fulness of time" (1:10) through and in Jesus Christ. Thus Christ is the mediator of God's saving plan. But there is yet another agent of this plan who figures very prominently in Ephesians, namely the Spirit. It is quite obvious from the way Paul speaks about the Spirit: *the* Spirit, *a* Spirit, *Holy* Spirit, *his* Spirit that he is thinking of a reality which belongs to God, which is distinct from man, but which is communicable to man – and in fact has been given to him.

In all discussion about the Spirit it is essential, at the outset, to be clear that we are considering a metaphor. Just like the terms "Father" and "Son", "Spirit" is a figurative term derived from human experience and used to describe a "divine", transcendant reality. The Spirit is real, does indeed exist, in the sense that the Christian experience being explained has an "objective" basis or cause. But this reality cannot be identified purely and simply with the literal meaning of the word "spirit" (any more than the reality of Father and Son can).

The main difficulty associated with an understanding of the Spirit is the extensiveness and vagueness of the term itself. We all know, basically, what "father" and "son" mean. But what about "spirit"? Even "father" and "son" are relative terms: father or son *of* someone. But "spirit" appears to be much less definite – we might say "completely" relative. This might also apply to "father" and "son" but at least we do know people who *are* fathers and sons, whereas we only know spirits *of* . . . . In the Old Testament "spirit" is associated with movement, power, activity and life. The Spirit of God is nothing other than God himself but considered as moving, actively powerful, alive and life-giving. It is a term, therefore, which expresses God's relationship with his creation. It does not attempt to describe God as he is "in himself". As a metaphor it is designed to describe and explain man's experience of God in his own life and in the world about him. This biblical background is obviously of prime importance for an appreciation of Paul's view of the Spirit.

Another difficulty presented by the "spirit" is that, even in the Bible, it is not only God who has one. Man, too, is endowed with a spirit – a point which is obvious, because God's "spirit" is the elevation to the "divine" sphere of what man experiences in his own world. This does mean, however, that it is very often difficult, impossible even, to decide whether, in a given passage, the term "spirit" refers to man or to God. Usually the context will clarify the issue, but sometimes (and this happens in Ephesians) the meaning remains ambiguous. Such ambiguity is itself important and often needs to be respected and preserved. For it is precisely in the realm of the "spirit" that, according to the Bible, man is most closely related, indeed "involved", with God. Perhaps the most telling text in this regard is Gen 2:7 where man is presented as being "inspired" with God's own "breath of life" (the term "breath" here in the Greek is a cognate of the word for "spirit"). According to the anthropology of this text, it is impossible to distinguish between man's spirit and God's spirit in man. The whole point of the account is that man is only truly human when he is "inspired" by, that is influenced profoundly by, God. We shall see that, with the Christological proviso, Paul's message in Ephesians is the same.

We can say that, according to Ephesians, "spirit" is the means by which the reality of salvation, that is the life of God himself, revealed in Christ, is *communicated* to men. Conversely, it is the means by which men participate in this life or the one condition under which they are able to make this life their own. Without the Spirit they would be like the clay of Gen 2:7 or the dry bones of Ezek 37, that is, lifeless. But with the Spirit they live, and this with God's own life. With hindsight we can consider both Gen 2:7 and Ezek 37 as prophetical in this regard. But the message of Ephesians is that the Spirit in question is the Spirit *of Jesus Christ* (even though Paul does not use this expression). In this respect the Johannine account of the risen Christ's appearance to his disciples is even more illuminating (Jn 20:19-23). In this passage Jesus does not only "breathe" the Holy Spirit upon his disciples, he also proclaims "peace" to them. The thought here is very similar to what we have in Eph 2:17-18.

Paul's use of the "spirit" metaphor evinces once again his efforts to explain his own Christian experience. The God whom he met in his conversion experience was indeed the God of his Jewish religion, the Lord of the Old Testament, but now manifesting himself in the man Jesus who is his "son", "word", "image". As a Christian, Paul would claim unhesitatingly that if you want to see God you must now look at Jesus; if you want to hear God you must listen to Jesus: he is the complete and ultimate revelaton of God. But Paul is also aware of his participation in this revelation. It was made to him, he has received it, he enjoys it. It is not

merely a fact external to himself. It is a real communication. God is active not only through and in Jesus but also
within him – Paul – personally. How can he conceptualize
and express this experience? Steeped as he is in the biblical
tradition, it is perfectly natural for him to exploit the motif
of the spirit. It is by the Spirit that God enables men to
receive, assimilate, interiorize, appropriate his revelation
that is Christ. Thus salvation involves a "trinity". It is
God the Father who takes the initiative in revealing his love
for men. This revelation is expressed Christ, his Word.
In speaking he also communicates his Spirit, by which men
can receive the Word and its effects. The relationship
between Spirit and Word is particularly intriguing. It can be
best understood by analogy with human oral communication. In order to speak, that is to utter a word, a sound, we
need breath (that is "spirit"). The more breath we have the
louder we are able to speak, the more we are able to make
ourselves heard. Word and breath are two sides of the same
reality. Moreover, try to separate the spoken word from the
breath. Paul himself suggests that the Spirit and the Word
of God are inseparable (6:17).

In other words, it is by the Spirit that all the blessings
of salvation are made accessible to man. This is suggested
already at the beginning of the *berakah* with the description
of the Father's blessing as "spiritual" (1:3). It is by the
Spirit that everything that God has accomplished in Christ
(1:3-13) becomes communicable to all other men. If all this
were not "spiritual" (in the biblical sense) it would remain
personal to him. Paul makes this idea explicit at the end
of his *berakah* with the mention of the Holy Spirit (1:13). By
this Spirit we not only enjoy the promises of salvation made
previously to Israel, but we also are able to realize the
holiness for which we have been chosen (1:4). This holiness
communicated by the Spirit is evoked again in 2:21,22 and
4:30. It is by "spirit" (here the term is ambiguous) that
wisdom and revelation are communicated (1:17). Much
more clearly, it is by God's Spirit that we benefit from God's

power (3:16). The Spirit is a principle of the unity realized by Christ between Jews and Gentiles (2:18), a unity which is an essential mark of the church (4:3,4). Indeed, the very mystery of Christ was made known to the apostles only through the Spirit (3:5). Ironically, although the Spirit might appear to arrive "ontologically" last on the scene of salvation (after the Father and the Son), in fact he comes first in our knowledge of this salvation. For it is only by the Spirit that we can hear the Word, just as it is only through the Word that we can hear the Father.

No theme is more important in Ephesians than that of prayer. It is very significant, therefore, that Paul should explicitly relate prayer with the Spirit (5:18,19; 6:18). Highly significant, too, that the one *offensive* arm in the whole divine panoply (6:10-17) should be the "Sword of the Spirit" (6:17). The Spirit is not only a condition of our receiving salvation. It is also an active principle within us, the means whereby we, as the body of Christ, continue and accomplish in ourselves and the rest of the universe his saving work. The Spirit is both the guarantee of our eventual success (1:14) and the means of achieving it.

The Trinity

There are several passages in Ephesians which present a clear "trinitarian structure", that is which show the "three": Father, Christ and Spirit acting in unison for our salvation (1:13-14; 1:17; 2:18; 2:22; 3:14-17; 4:4-6; 5:18-20). Consideration of these passages, along with what we have already seen concerning the Father, Christ and the Spirit, permits us to say that salvation means that the Father unites us to himself, through Christ, in the Spirit. Thus salvation is itself trinitarian or – to be more precise – "quaternarian". For it comprises *four* elements: the Father, Christ, the Spirit *and* us, that is the redeemed universe. There would be no salvation without us, that is without our acceptance of God's saving plan. From what Paul says about Christ and the Spirit, it is clear that although they are related to us (and, according to Paul, even God is related to us) they are, nevertheless, as distinct from us as the Father himself is. They are *of* God in a sense not verifiable of creation. In this sense they are "divine". We must recall immediately, however, that the very names (and in the Bible the "name" describes the reality) by which Paul knows them designate creation as their *raison d'être*. Moreover, the whole point of salvation is precisely what we might call the "divinisation" of man, the transformation of men into the Father's children. This is possible only through Christ and in the Spirit because they are "divine". More exactly, if we wish to recapture the train of Paul's thought, we ought to say: since *we* have been "divinised" through Christ in the Spirit, then *they* must be divine. Paul would not know *about* Christ and the Spirit if he did not know *them*, that is if he did not experience them as the causes of his new relationship with God. His knowledge of them is the knowledge of what they are *to him*.

It would be just as unjustifiable, therefore, to dispute that in Ephesians Father, Son (4:13) and Spirit are "divine" as it would be to claim that they appear there as three distinct "persons" in the sense of later trinitarian theology. What is certain is that here, as elsewhere in the New Testament, God is presented as acting as "trinity". But precisely *what* these three are it is not possible to say. As Augustine put it: "Quid tres, sed tres quid?" – "There are three something, but three what?"

In other words, in Ephesians Paul is not concerned about God as he is in himself. He is interested only in the God "who has blessed us" (1:3). Nor does he intend to describe or explain God's interior life, the inter-relationship between Father, Son and Spirit. His sole aim is to outline the "mystery" of our relationship with God, to explain what God has done for us. Not that he has made a deliberate option in this regard, choosing between an abstract, "ontological" theology and the concrete, "existential" one. The former was an unknown possibility, reserved for the future, as far as Paul was concerned. The "stuff" of his theology is the Christian experience which he seeks to communicate, foster, protect and explain. It is in doing this that he has produced, almost unconsciously, the material for other theologies.

Thanksgiving.
1:15-16.

[15]For this reason, because I have heard of your faith in the Lord Jesus and your love toward all the saints, [16]I do not cease to give thanks for you, remembering you in my prayers.

Paul has hardly paused for breath when he launches himself into another prayer. This time it is a prayer of thanksgiving. The motive for this thanksgiving is the faith and love of his readers. We have already seen what Paul means by faith (v.1). The love in question is doubtless the generosity shown by the readers in contributing to the collection which Paul had organised for the benefit of the "saints", that is the faithful of the Palestinian churches. It would be impossible to exaggerate the importance of this collection in Paul's religious development. It figures fairly prominently in his letters (Gal 2:10; 1 Cor 16:1-4; 2 Cor 8-9; Rom 15:25-29). It was certainly one of the motives of his ardent evangelisation of the East. But – most importantly – it was the tangible proof of the efficacy of the gospel. The love shown by the Gentile churches in responding to Paul's appeal was visible evidence that they had grasped the meaning of the gospel of love. Their acceptance of the gospel was not only in word but also in deed. Their unity with their Jewish brethren was not only by faith but also by love. It was by giving them a share in their material blessings that they became participants in the Jewish inheritance (v.14). "Saints" was probably a title enjoyed firstly by the Jewish Christians of Jerusalem. Through their love, however, the Gentile Christians were united with the Jewish Christians of Palestine and so became "saints" themselves (v.1). The collection had the effect of welding together all the individual churches, turning them into one universal church united by faith and love. It was without a doubt Paul's collection experience that enabled him to consider the church not only as the local assembly but also as the universal community of all believers.

But Paul does not consider that love, any more than faith (v.1), is a mere response on men's part to God's gift. Love, like faith, is itself a gift. It may indeed be a response, but it is a God-given response. The love which Paul has in mind is God's love which, as he puts it in Romans "has been poured into our hearts through the Holy Spirit which has been given us" (Rom 5:5). It is a fruit of the Holy Spirit which we have received in baptism (v.13). Thus it is the motive for thanksgiving. In thanking God for his readers' faith and love Paul is acknowledging that these are God's gifts. Both faith and love are God's own activity within men. Even the prayer of thanksgiving is itself a gift (as indeed is all prayer for Paul: Rom 8:26-27), in so far as the motive of the thanksgiving is revealed by God. In fact, as far as Paul is concerned, every aspect of our relationship with God is grace.

At this point it is worth noting the importance of prayer in Paul's experience of the apostolate. Paul is here not merely praying out loud, as he was in his *berakah*. He is now praying "for" or on behalf of his readers. Prayer for others, especially intercessory prayer, is as vital an aspect of the

Christian religion as it is misunderstood. A reflection on what Paul says here may help us to appreciate its real meaning. Firstly, it is evident from the following verses that Paul is really interceding for his readers. He is, therefore, asking for something on their behalf. This request presupposes that God is both willing and able to accede to it. Indeed, the explicit description of this prayer as a thanksgiving suggests that it is good as answered. Secondly, Paul is not only praying for his readers. He is also letting them know that he is praying for them. His prayer is addressed just as much to them as it is to God. It is a revelation of what God is willing and able to do in them and for them. Paul's prayer, therefore, is a facet of his apostolate. It is a way of preaching and teaching. Thirdly, this prayer expresses the apostle's personal involvement in his mission. He is not an indifferent "neutral" instrument in the communication of the gospel. He is personally committed to God's saving work. He really wants for his readers what God wills for them. By his prayer he actually shares in God's saving will. Prayer is the expression of his concern and love for his readers. It follows from all this that prayer, for Paul, is designed to effect a change not in God but in men. According to Paul, God is Father, the "Giver" *par excellence*, love itself. He has no need to be notified or reminded of his creatures' requirements and desires. On the contrary, it is we who need to become aware of the salvation which God has achieved in us. It is prayer which makes this change possible – our own prayer, in so far as this prayer represents our openness to God's activity; the prayer of others, in so far as we are attentive to the message contained in this prayer. The following verses will make this very clear.

Intercession.
1:17-19.

[17]that the God of our Lord Jesus Christ, the Father of glory, may give you a spirit of wisdom and of revelation

in the knowledge of him, [18]having the eyes of your hearts
enlightened, that you may know what is the hope to
which he has called you, what are the riches of his
glorious inheritance in the saints, [19]and what is the
immeasurable greatness of his power in us who believe,
according to the working of his great might [which he
accomplished in Christ].

In his opening *berakah* Paul has described God's plan
of salvation and – to this extent – he has given his readers a
knowledge of it. But in this prayer he implies that such an
objective description of the "mystery" is not sufficient
to impart a proper knowledge. This is possible only as a gift
and by the activity of God himself. The knowledge in
question is something other than intellectual. It is knowledge in the biblical sense of intimate experience. This
experience is the experience of God himself, of our final
destiny and of his present power at work in us. The most
fundamental experience is that of God as the "Father of
glory". This leads necessarily to the experience our inheritance of this glory, both as already acquired in baptism and
as the object of our hope for the end of time. In fact we are
assured of the final and complete acquisition of our inheritance by our experience of the power which God has already
exerted on us in bringing us to faith.

Description of God's Power.
1:20 – 2:10.

GOD'S POWER IN CHRIST.
1:20-23.

[according to the working of his great might] [20]which
he accomplished in Christ when he raised him from the
dead and made him sit at his right hand in the heavenly

places, ²¹far above all rule and authority and power and
dominion, and above every name that is named, not
only in this age but also in that which is to come; ²²and
he has put all things under his feet and has made him the
head over all things for the church, ²³which is his body,
the fulness of him who fills all in all.

In order to avoid misunderstanding radically Paul's
thought here, it is necessary to notice that this section on
God's power in Christ is relative to his main concern which
is with God's power in or towards believers. He is describing
the power which the believer ought to experience in his own
life. As pregnant as these two verses may be in themselves,
therefore, they should not be understood as absolute state-
ments about what God has done in Christ so much as illus-
trations of what God has done for us. Christ's resurrection
is a central theme in Paul but it is remarkable that he never
considers it in itself, that is as an event which concerns
Christ himself. He always introduces it to justify or to
explain some other facet of salvation which he considers
to be the more important.

In the present instance Paul refers to God's raising and
exaltation of Christ as *the* paradigm of God's power
towards believers. The mention of the "heavenly places"
recalls vv.3 and 10 and reminds us that the whole purpose
of this Christ-event was salvific, that is that all men should
be in Christ. Against the background of the early church's
belief in the resurrection of Christ, Ps 110:1 and primitive
cosmology (v.10), Paul shows that God's power revealed
in Christ was absolute and limitless.

Paul now (vv.22-23) enlists the help of Ps 8:6 in his effort
to express his understanding of the Christ-event. This psalm
originally referred to man in general and v.8 celebrated
his God-given dominion over the rest of the animal world
(vv.7-8). But Paul here applies it to Christ who, by being
raised and exalted (v.20), has had the universe placed
beneath his feet. This is an imaginative way of expressing

Christ's excellence, a variation of the theme already enunciated in v.20 where the application of Ps 110:1 to Christ brought out his unique relationship with God. The reference to Ps 8 illustrates more the relationship of Christ to creation.

The image of Christ having all things under his feet naturally leads to the other image of his being the "head" of the universe. In its turn, this image corresponds admirably to Paul's description of God's plan (v.10). In fact, Christ's resurrection, together with his session at God's right hand and his supremacy over the universe, is for a purpose. And this purpose is the creation of the church. It is the church that now becomes the focal point of salvation.

In his previous letters Paul refers to the local community as the "church". In this letter the term refers no longer to such communities, but to the universal assembly of all believers who are united in Christ by their faith and love (v.15). It is this church that is the "body" of Christ. In Paul's anthropology "body" is not just a part of man, distinct from his soul or spirit. For the Jew that Paul was man *is* a "body". Thus the metaphor of body applied to the church suggests that the church *is* Christ visibly and tangibly present in the world.

In earlier letters Paul has described the church (that is the local church) as Christ's body (1 Cor 12:12-31; Rom 12:4-5). Only there he did not make any distinction between the "head" and the "body". His present concern with the cosmic aspect of the Christ-event has led him to make this distinction. Now Christ is seen as the heavenly "head" and the church as his earthly "body". Nevertheless, the "whole Christ" – to use Augustine's phrase – is both "head" and "body". A "head" without a "body" is nonsensical, and *vice versa*. The value of the differentiation is that it stresses both Christ's primacy and the fact that the universe is moving "upwards" to Christ. The relationship of the church to Christ is a double one: on the one hand, the church receives all its life, energy and inspiration from God through Christ; on the other hand, it is directed towards him.

Paul explicitly mentions the church's complementary character. As his "body" the church is Christ's "fulness" or "completion". Without the church Christ would not be whole. Such an apparently audacious view follows necessarily from the fact that the Christ-event was designed to bring about men's salvation. This salvation is the re-unification of the universe, and especially all men, in Christ. The church is the realisation of this re-unification. If there were no church there would be no actual salvation. God's work in Christ would be fruitless.

What Paul seems to be saying in these very dense verses is this: by raising Christ from the dead and seating him at his right hand, God has "filled" the universe with Christ and made him its Lord. In itself, this reality of Christ's omnipresence and supremacy is invisible, intangible and non-experiential. It is a "mystery". But, in fact, it has been revealed. And the church is precisely its revelation. Just as a man is present to the world in his "body", so Christ is present to the world in his "body" the church. It is only in, through and by the church that the reality of salvation can be seen and experienced. The church is both the end and the means of salvation. God's plan is to make one, vast "church" or community of creation. Until this plan is finally accomplished, the church's role is to be – and (because it is Christ's "body") be *seen* to be – the "first-fruits" of universal harmony.

GOD'S POWER IN BELIEVERS.
2:1-10.

> **2** And you he made alive, when you were dead through the trespasses and sins ²in which you once walked, following the course of this world, following the prince of the power of the air, the spirit that is now at work in the sons of disobedience. ³Among these we all once lived in the passions of our flesh, following the desires of body and mind, and so we were by nature children of wrath,

like the rest of mankind. [4]But God, who is rich in mercy, out of the great love with which he loved us, [5]even when we were dead through our trespasses, made us alive together with Christ (by grace you have been saved), [6]and raised us up with him, and made us sit with him in the heavenly places in Christ Jesus, [7]that in the coming ages he might show the immeasurable riches of his grace in kindness toward us in Christ Jesus. [8]For by grace you have been saved through faith; and this is not your own doing, it is the gift of God—[9]not because of works, lest any man should boast. [10]For we are his workmanship, created in Christ Jesus for good works, which God prepared beforehand, that we should walk in them.

From Death to Life.
2:1-3.

The very same power (1:19) which God has exercised on Christ (1:20-23) he has also put to work in the faithful. As in the case of Christ this power is essentially life-giving. Paul is here thinking particularly of his Gentile readers (1:13) who, before their conversion, were totally outside the community of salvation (1:11-12). Then they were spiritually dead because of their "trespasses and sins" (1:8) which themselves denoted a certain pattern of behaviour dictated by a "world" and a "spirit" inimical to God. Here, again, Paul is using mythical language, but his message is clear: before they heard and accepted the gospel the Gentile Christians were as dead in their sins as Christ was in his grave before he was raised by God. This is another way of expressing the purely gratuitous character of salvation (Rom 5:6-11).

Paul draws a distinction between the Gentile Christians and those who are still influenced by the (evil) spirit, but it is noticeable that he refers to these as "the sons of disobedience". The dualism which Paul has in mind is a moral or spiritual one, not a metaphysical one. If men are under the influence of the (evil) spirit, this is not through no fault of their own. It is because they are disobedient, that is they have not "heard" the "word of truth" (v.13), in the biblical sense of submitting oneself to the word of God. Thus the relationship between "the sons of disobedience" and the (evil) spirit is the antithesis of the relationship between the faithful and the Holy Spirit (1:13). The faithful are "the sons of obedience". It is by obeying God's life-giving word that they have passed from the death of sin to the life of grace.

But it is not only Gentile Christians who were once "sons of disobedience" (v.2). "We" (v.3), that is Jewish Christians (1:11-12), were also "dead", though not so much through the influence of an evil spirit as through "the desires of body and mind". The expression "children of wrath" is, like "sons of disobedience", a semitism. It means that the Jewish Christians, before their conversion, were deserving of God's "wrath", that is the attitude which he has towards sin. Once more, we see that this state is a moral or spiritual one, not a metaphysical one: it is caused by our desires. Thus it is "by nature" not in the sense that we were born into it, but in the sense that it was an established fact. What Paul is saying is that, as far as the radical need of salvation is concerned, there was no difference between Jews and Gentiles. All were sinners and, without God's grace, were dead men (Rom 3:22-23).

God, Rich in Mercy.
2:4-7.

According to Paul, our salvation is not a matter of making "reparation" for sin, of "satisfying" the demands of God's justice, of "placating" his "anger" (v.4). It is purely and simply a matter of God's love. This is evident from the fact that while we were "dead" in the very offences which we committed against God, he has "made us alive".

He has accepted us *as* enemies and reconciled us to himself (Rom 5:8). Thus our salvation is a pure gift or "grace", completely unmerited and undeserved.

We have already seen that, for Paul, our salvation is achieved only *in* Christ (1:1). He now focuses our attention on another dimension of this salvation: it also achieved *with* Christ. What God has accomplished in Christ (1:20-22) was not for him alone but also and indeed *primarily* for all other men. It is significant that Paul speaks not of the resurrection and exaltation of *Jesus* but of *Christ*. Obviously for Paul Jesus and Christ are one and the same person (v.6). But there is, in fact, a difference of meaning between the two names. "Jesus" denotes the individual man who lived and died at a particular point of time in the past. "Christ" denotes this same person in his role as the mediator of God's saving plan for all other men. Now it was by raising and exalting Jesus that God achieved *our* salvation. In this sense we can speak about Jesus "becoming" Christ by his resurrection and exaltation (Rom 1:3-4). In other words, the very term "Christ" implies a relationship. Just as the term "Messiah" implies a messianic community, so the term "Christ" implies the church of Christ. A Christ without members is as unthinkable as a "head" without a "body" (1:22-23). All this means that God, in raising and exalting Jesus, has also raised and exalted us with him. Thus the imagery of 1:20-23 should not be pushed too far. For there is a sense in which the church is not destined to remain forever "below" Christ; it is also called to "sit with him" in the heavenly places, to reign over the rest of creation with him. Such a view of the Christ-event coincides with the original meaning of Ps 8 (1:22).

Obviously resurrection and exaltation are verified of Jesus, at the present time, in a way that does not apply to us: he has personally died and now enjoys the relationship with God which still lies in the future, as far as we are concerned. Nevertheless, Paul here speaks about our own resurrection and exaltation not as a future hope but as a past event: God "*raised* us up with him, and *made* us sit with him in the heavenly places". This past is probably a reference to the event of baptism, by which the Christian is considered to die and rise with Christ (Rom 6:4). In any case, the all-important point is that there is a sense in which we already enjoy the new life and heavenly triumph of Christ. In fact, taking a cue from 1:22-23, we could say that it is Christ who enjoys his new life and heavenly triumph in us, his "body".

As in 1:6, Paul here (v.7) stresses that the work of salvation is a revelation of God's grace. In its present existence the church, being the risen and exalted "body" of Christ, is intended by God to be the visible and tangible manifestation of his grace. Later in this letter Paul will suggest some ways in which this vocation may be realised.

Saved Through Faith.
2:8-10.

It is through faith that men receive God's grace. Here Paul touches on the theme which he elaborated at great length in both Romans and Galatians: it is only by faith in Christ that men are saved. In these letters Paul was intent on opposing this faith to works of the Jewish law. In the present context, however, his point is that this faith itself is a gift of God. It is not men's work but God's and just as much a grace as salvation itself. Thus, according to Paul, salvation is not a matter of a partnership between men and God, with God offering the gift and man receiving it with this own effort. Both the gift and its reception are grace. It is less a matter of man himself receiving the gift than of God receiving it within man. And this applies as much to the whole of the Christians' moral life as it does to the act of faith. Even our "good works" are not so much the response which *we* make to God's initiative as the expression of God's creative power within us. Truly, according to Paul, man is the *milieu divin*, the sphere of God's activity.

The Union of Jews and Gentiles.
2:11-22.

We must not forget that Paul is still engaged in the prayer of intercession which he began in 1:17. This is a prayer that his readers should appreciate God's power at work within them. To help them to do this Paul repeatedly describes the known effects of this power. Thus he now turns to one of its more dramatic effects: the union of Jews and Gentiles (1:11-14).

THE SITUATION BEFORE CHRIST.
2:11-12.

> [11]Therefore remember that at one time you Gentiles in the flesh, called the uncircumcision by what is called the circumcision, which is made in the flesh by hands— [12]remember that you were at that time separated from Christ, alienated from the commonwealth of Israel, and strangers to the covenants of promise, having no hope and without God in the world.

Paul now addresses the Gentile Christians directly, reminding them of the hopeless situation in which they were before the Christ-event. At the same time he assigns a positive role to Israel, while intimating to his Jewish readers that this was not due to circumcision, since circumcision is a matter of the flesh and not of the Spirit (1:3,13).

CHRIST'S UNIFYING WORK.
2:13-18.

> [13]But now in Christ Jesus you who once were far off have been brought near in the blood of Christ. [14]For he is our peace, who has made us both one, and has broken down the dividing wall of hostility, [15]by abolishing in his flesh the law of commandments and ordinances, that he might create in himself one new man in place of the

two, so making peace, [16]and might reconcile us both to God in one body through the cross, thereby bringing the hostility to an end. [17]And he came and preached peace to you who were far off and peace to those who were near; [18]for through him we both have access in one Spirit to the Father.

Previously (1:20-2:10) Paul concentrated on Christ's resurrection and exaltation. Now he concentrates on his death and significantly it is Christ who is the subject of saving activity. He is no longer the one who is raised and exalted but the one who unites, breaks down, abolishes, creates, makes peace, reconciles and brings hostility to an end.

Paul sees Christ's death, here evoked by "blood" (v.13) and "the cross" (v.16), as a unifying force. Before Christ mankind was divided into two sectors: the Jews and the Gentiles, the divisive factor being the Jewish law itself. Now Christ died because of, or according to, the Jewish law. His death appeared to be a victory of this law. But his resurrection vindicated him and showed the inefficacy of the law. Thus by his death (seen in the light of his resurrection) he annulled the law and abolished all the radical differences between men. At the same time he brought about a new, profound unity between all men. He has become the beginning of a new humanity. Previously (2:4) we saw that Paul does not consider salvation as man's work in any way. Here, however, he depicts Christ as "reconciling" humanity to God, thus bringing to an end not only the hostility between men but also that between men and God. The metaphor of "reconciliation" is one which would appeal particularly to Christians of Gentile origin. Christ has reconciled us to God "in one body" in two senses: on the one hand, it is in his physical body on the cross, that is through his death, that he has reconciled us; on the other hand, it is in his metaphorical body, that is in the church (1:23), that he has done this. As we have already seen (1:5), it is the death of Christ, considered as a revelation of God's love, that has brought men together. By this union they are not only united with one another but also, *ipso facto*, reconciled with God. According to Paul, Christ's death is salvific or reconciliatory in so far as it is revelatory: it manifests God's love which, in its turn, moves men to love one another and so participate in this love. It is in this way that they pass from a state of enmity or hatred to the condition of love. This is what Paul means by reconciliation.

In vv.17-18 Paul could be referring to the whole of Christ's work (including his earthly preaching), seen as the accomplishment of Is 57:19: "Peace, peace, to the far and to the near, says the Lord". But he is more likely evoking the risen Christ's appearance to his disciples described in Jn 20:19-23. In any case, the "peace" offered to the exiles (Is 57:19) and that bestowed on the disciples (Jn 20:19-21) is more than a greeting. The "peace" in question is the *shalom* which denotes the fulness of all that is good. In the Bible it is a synonym of salvation. This "peace" is not just the cessation of hostility, effected by Christ's death (v.16). It is the complete happiness accomplished by his resurrection and communicated to Gentiles and Jews alike in the Spirit. Paul sees Christ as the mediator of the Spirit. By his death on the cross he has created a new man (v.15). By his resurrection he has become not only "a living being" (like the first Adam) but a "life-giving spirit" (1 Cor 15:45). Once more (1:3) the trinitarian structure of Paul's thought is very clear: all men have access *to* the Father, *through* Christ, *in* the Spirit.

According to Paul, the essence of salvation is the realisation, made possible through Christ, that God is Father and that all men are his children. It is this realisation that provides the only true basis for the unity of mankind. As Paul sees it, this unity is indeed "spiritual" in that it transcends any natural or man-made ties. But it is also "bodily" in so far as it is manifest fully only in the church. This church for Paul is more than a "denomination", a group characterised by anything which is not universally human. It is mankind itself, united by the one "badge" of love, that is the love revealed in Christ (1:15).

THE PRESENT SITUATION.
2:19-22.

> [19] So then you are no longer strangers and sojourners, but you are fellow citizens with the saints and members of the household of God, [20] built upon the foundation of the apostles and prophets, Christ Jesus himself being the chief cornerstone, [21] in whom the whole structure is joined together and grows into a holy temple in the Lord; [22] in whom you also are built into it for a dwelling place of God in the Spirit.

Through their baptism the Gentiles' previous position, as described in 2:11-12, has been completely reversed. Now they share all the prerogatives once reserved for Israel. This means that Israel, considered as a distinct social entity, no longer has a special role to play in God's saving plan. The "true" Israel, the "real" holy society is the universal church, understood in the sense just described by Paul (vv.17-18). God's "household" includes the whole of mankind.

The image of the "household" leads, almost imperceptibly, to that of the "building". It is interesting to note that the community of Qumran considered itself to be a spiritual building, constructed by its fidelity to the law of Moses. Paul uses this metaphor, probably because it is ideal for bringing out the idea that the church is a very carefully planned, designed and structured society. It has been deliberately willed by God. It is not some kind of "club" which men have devised for themselves. But for Paul the basis of this edifice is not the Mosaic law. It is "the apostles and prophets" or, more precisely, the preaching and teaching which these have conveyed (1:13). In this context, "prophets" could refer to the Old Testament prophets, but it more probably refers to the prophets/teachers within the church. Christian believing begins with preaching and teaching, but it achieves its climax with Christ, in the sense that Christ is seen to be the "head", that is the point towards which the whole of faith is moving and from which it receives its consistency. Thus Paul is not here contradicting what he held in 1 Cor 3:11: "For no other foundation can any one lay than that which is laid, which is Jesus Christ". In Ephesians, he is concerned with the headship or supremacy of Christ (1:22-23). It is more appropriate, therefore, that he should speak of Christ here as the "cornerstone" of the church. This is just an application of the "head" theme to a "building".

But the church is not *any kind* of building; it is a "holy" building or temple, and this "in" Christ. It is, therefore, no longer a question of Christ being merely the "cornerstone", that is a part (albeit an important part) of the whole building. He is now depicted as *the* temple itself, into whom the baptised are "built". In fact, according to the early church, it is Christ himself who, by his resurrection (Jn 2:21-22), is God's true temple, that is the "place" where God both lives and is worshipped. By their baptism, however, Christians are "inserted" into Christ, becoming members of his body and stones of his temple. The metaphors of body and temple are closely associated and, to a great extent, complementary. If the image of body expresses the profound and "vital" character of the union between the church and Christ, that of temple expresses the divine and cultic character of this union. Paul wants his readers to understand that God lives within them and is worshipped by them, in so far as they are "in" Christ. If John can say "The word became flesh and built its tabernacle among us" (Jn 1:14), Paul maintains that, by receiving this word (1:13), we become a part of this "tabernacle" or temple.

As in v.18, Paul expresses himself in "trinitarian" terms. God the Father dwells (and is worshipped) in the church "in" Christ and "in" the Spirit. It is only because the church is in Christ that it has the Spirit of God.

NOTE:

Christian Existence

By receiving the "gospel" which is God's word in the "form" of Christ, the believer undergoes a radical conversion, a spiritual renewal, and enters into a new kind of existence. This is entirely the fruit of God's infallibly efficacious word which brings about precisely what it means. In speaking Christ to men, God quite simply makes them Christ. Christ is God's "truth". If men are to recognize this truth, it is not only their minds but their total reality that must be conformed to it: they have to *be*, to *exist in* Christ. To apply Tillich's famous phrase to a slightly different context from its original one: Christ must be the "ground of our being". Existence *in* Christ is one of the major themes of Ephesians. We have already seen something of how Christ is the mediator or the medium of salvation. What we now need to look at a little more closely is the "existence" or "being" aspect of salvation.

It is important to realize that Paul sees salvation, first and foremost, as a matter of *being*. God's plan for men is that they should enjoy a new kind of existence – the existence of God himself. Paul makes this perfectly clear in two passages of his *berakah*: ". . . he chose us in him before the foundation of the world, that we should *be* holy and blameless before him" (1:5); ". . . we who first hoped in Christ have been destined and appointed *to be* for the praise of his glory" (1:12). In the latter passage the R.S.V. translates the original Greek verb "to be" by "to live", which may appear to make better sense but in fact distorts Paul's real meaning. Later in his letter Paul will show the importance of "living" or, more precisely, "behaving" for the praise of God's glory. For the moment he is more concerned with man's being, what we would call his "ontological status".

In having God bestow a new kind of existence upon man, Paul automatically spotlights man's paradoxical and anomalous situation. For, on the one hand, this new existence is a grace, a perfectly free gift, something to which man has no right, which is in no way demanded by human nature. Paul expresses this purely gratuitous character of salvaton in various ways. He refers to it explicitly as a "grace" (2:5,8). By describing it as a "resurrection", he intimates that it is utterly impossible for us to achieve on our own (2:1f). But it is above all in his insistence on the role of prayer, particularly intercessory prayer, that this idea becomes clear: salvation is not only the object of thanksgiving, that is "eucharist", it also needs to be ardently requested. On the other hand, left without this free gift of salvation, man remains in a deprived and subservient state, "by nature children of wrath" (2:3), "following the prince of the power of the air" (2:2), "following the desires of body and mind" (2:3). Paul presents salvation as a real liberation and as true human fulfilment. The new existence *in* Christ is contrasted and opposed to man's existence without Christ. The latter state is considered to be an alienation from God (2:12) and yet "natural" to man. To be completely human, man needs God. But God gives himself to many only as a perfectly free gift. We are back at the anthropology of Gen 2:7.

Paul calls this new existence "holiness" and "sonship". According to the Bible, only God is "holy" in the strict sense of this term. Entymologically, "holiness" means "apartness", "separateness", "otherness", "transcendence". It thus describes the transcendence of God with regard to his creatures, and underlines the fact that they are not "divine". In itself, it does not denote good moral behaviour. But also, according to the Bible, God communicates his "holiness" to men, that is he makes them "holy". This applies particularly to the Israelites who are known as the "saints". Paul sees this prerogative as now being transferred to the baptised (1:1). All Christians are already "saints" because they now exist *in* Christ. This "sanctity" does not directly indicate good moral behaviour. Nor is it acquired by "good works". It is a condition of being, a participation in the very existence of God.

"Sonship", like "holiness", is a term which designates a state of being. More precisely, it indicates a relationship. By our baptism we really *are* God's children and are related to him as to a Father.

According to Paul, the new existence which God has afforded us *in* Christ is a present reality. We are already "holy", already God's children and, as such, already united to form God's "household" (2:19) and his "dwelling place" (2:22). Moreover, the mere fact that we *are* a "holy temple" (2:21) means that, by our very existence, we give glory to God. For the *raison d'être* of a temple is worship. Worship is not accessory to our Christian existence, a mere function which we perform. We worship God by *being* what we are by baptism. The Father is "glorified" in the existence of his children.

This present reality is, however, capable of development and growth. The "Holy Spirit", which is its principle (1:13) is the "guarantee of our inheritance until we acquire possession of it, to the praise of his glory" (1:14). Thus the Christian existence is characterized by both an "already" and a "not yet". For we have not yet attained "to the unity of the faith and of the knowledge of the Son of God, to mature manhood, to the measure of the stature of the fulness of Christ" (4:13). This future aspect of salvation is expressed poignantly by the image of God's "call" (1:18; 4:1). The same divine word which makes us God's children is also a "call", that is an invitation to *become* God's children. But this "becoming" is also an effect of the word itself. God's invitation does not have R.S.V.P. written on it. It is charged with its own reply. According to Paul, man is not *free* to accept or reject this invitation. Rather, he is *freed* to accept it. It is God's word, addressed to him in Christ, that liberates him and enables him to become God's son. The continual process of filiation and sanctification in which we are involved, from our reception of the "gospel" onwards, is the work of God's word within us.

Intercession.
3:1-19.

All that Paul has said since 1:20 has been a continuation of his intercessory prayer which he began in 1:17. But now, as if to remind his readers that he is still praying for them, he repeats the formula "for this reason" (3:1; 1:15) which expresses the motivation for his prayer. The prayer of intercession will end only in 3:19. And, before this, Paul will take the opportunity to describe the "mystery" of salvation yet again.

3 For this reason I, Paul, a prisoner for Christ Jesus on behalf of you Gentiles—²assuming that you have heard of the stewardship of God's grace that was given to me for you, ³how the mystery was made known to me by revelation, as I have written briefly. ⁴When you read this you can perceive my insight into the mystery of Christ, ⁵which was not made known to the sons of men in other generations as it has now been revealed to his holy apostles and prophets by the Spirit; ⁶that is, how the Gentiles are fellow heirs, members of the same body, and partakers of the promise in Christ Jesus through the gospel.

⁷Of this gospel I was made a minister according to the gift of God's grace which was given me by the working of his power. ⁸To me, though I am the very least of all the saints, this grace was given, to preach to the Gentiles the unsearchable riches of Christ, ⁹and to make all men see what is the plan of the mystery hidden for ages in God who created all things; ¹⁰that through the church the manifold wisdom of God might now be made known to the principalities and powers in the heavenly places. ¹¹This was according to the eternal purpose which he has realized in Christ Jesus our Lord, ¹²in whom we have boldness and confidence of access through our faith in him. ¹³So I ask you to to lose heart over what I am suffering for you, which is your glory.

¹⁴For this reason I bow my knees before the Father, ¹⁵from whom every family in heaven and on earth is named, ¹⁶that according to the riches of his glory he may grant you to be strengthened with might through his Spirit in the inner man, ¹⁷and that Christ may dwell in your hearts through faith; that you, being rooted and grounded in love, ¹⁸may have power to comprehend with all the saints what is the breadth and length and height and depth, ¹⁹and to know the love of Christ which surpasses knowledge, that you may be filled with all the fullness of God.

The Mystery.
3:1-6.

Addressing himself principally to Christians of Gentile origin (2:11), Paul claims that he is in prison particularly because of his fidelity to his mission of evangelisation of the Gentiles. This idea leads him to digress into a description of this mission. With consummate discretion, he reminds his readers that he is merely the administrator of God's grace, the "mystery" or plan of which has been revealed to him. He intends all that he has written so far (especially 1:3-14; 1:20-2:10; 2:11-22) to be an indication of his grasp of this "mystery".

As Paul has already stressed (1:9), the "mystery" is unattainable by unaided human reason. It is the object of God's special revelation and the beneficiaries of this revelation are the "apostles and prophets" (2:20). God makes this revelation "by the Spirit", that is by giving his instruments a share in his own saving life (vv.4-5). Paul counts himself among those who are the founder members of the church (2:20). V.6 puts the "mystery" in a nutshell, as far as the Gentiles are concerned. We have already met its main ingredients: inheritance (1:14), membership of Christ's body (1:28), participation in the promise (1:13), all this being accomplished "in" Christ (1:1) through the gospel (1:13). By now the reader should feel that he is in very familiar territory. This is because Paul is an excellent teacher and so is able to inculcate his message by frequent repetition without, however, lulling his readers to sleep.

Minister of the Gospel.
3:7-13.

Just as the "mystery" contained in the gospel is attainable only by revelation, so the apostolate is itself a pure gift. Paul is only a "minister", that is a "servant" of the gospel, a mere instrument or channel through which God himself works. He did not volunteer for the apostolate; he was "called" to it (v.7).

But this "call" does not make Paul spiritually or morally superior to the other members of God's new people. The situation of the apostle is paradoxical. Although he is spiritually poor he is entrusted with the preaching of the "unsearchable riches of Christ" (v.8). Wealth is an object of men's desires and aspirations. Paul claims that they will find the fulfilment of these desires and aspirations in Christ. In speaking of "unsearchable" riches, Paul is mixing his metaphors, since "to search" here refers to the investigating activity of the mind. He is, in fact, referring again to the "mystery" which he has been called to transmit to men.

The mention of God's creative power serves to remind the readers of the purely gratuitous character of his saving plan (v.9). The God who saves the universe is exactly the same God who created it. Thus God does not *need* the universe. If he wills to save it, this can only be of his own completely free initiative. Furthermore, since he is the Creator, he not only *wills* to save; he is also *able* to do so. Indeed, as Paul has already intimated (2:10), salvation is a facet of creation. For him God's plan is a plan not only of salvation, but also of creation. The universe is fully created only when it is saved (1:10).

Here in v.10, as in 1:22, the church is the end and purpose of God's saving plan. It is through this church – Christ's visible and tangible body – that God's wisdom is revealed. It is, therefore, essentially a *saving* wisdom, one which concerns human fulfilment. The church is God's master-piece, the *raison d'être* of the Christ event-itself (1:22). As Christ's body, it makes his presence felt throughout the whole of creation, including the "principalities and powers in the heavenly places". Like "rule", "authority", "power" and "dominion" mentioned in 1:21, these "principalities and powers" are categories of non-human, spiritual beings, considered by Paul's contemporaries as superior to men and inhabiting "the heavenly places". It is possible that some Christians of Gnostic bent saw Christ himself as the incarnation of one of these beings. Paul has already rejected such an interpretation of Christ (1:20-23). He now maintains that not only Christ but also the church – Christ's body – has supremacy over the universe. In this sense, it is not only the "head" (1:20) that is in the "heavenly places", but also the "body". Christ's resurrection and exaltation have signalled the mastery of all men over creation, provided they are united in him and form the church.

If the church is the manifestation of God's plan for his universe, it follows that all men should be able, and have the right, to see this plan in fact. In speaking of "church", Paul has a very concrete reality in mind. He is referring to the visible and tangible unity of all believers and –eventually – all men in Christ. This is the only church which will ever be able to reveal fully God's saving plan.

Paul's commission to preach the gospel was not a divine after-thought but itself a part of God's eternal plan (v.11). The apostolate is integral to the Christ-event, being a function of the "total Christ". The preaching of the gospel is not the mere recalling of a past event. It is the repeated actualization of this event, by which Christ becomes really present to every generation.

The conviction that the apostolate is part and parcel of God's saving plan is the motive of Paul's unbounded boldness and confidence (v.12). His present imprisonment should, therefore, not depress his readers. On the contrary, they should see it as the climax of his mission as a member of the Christ who achieved salvation through suffering. This suffering, too, is part of God's universal plan and, especially if it is to culminate in death, can only be for the Gentiles' benefit (v.13). Over the years Paul has come to view apparent obstacles and set-backs positively, indeed as blessings in disguise (2 Cor 2:10). According to Paul the gospel progresses not despite difficulties but precisely because of them.

I Bow My Knees.
3:14-19.

Paul has digressed somewhat since 3:1, but now he returns to his principal theme: that of intercession (v.14). As in 1:15, he is informing his readers that he is praying for them. This has the effect of assuring them that he is concerned about them. Such a concern for others is already an important fruit of Christ's love. But, more importantly, by such a stress on his intercessory prayer, Paul is intimating that the progress in the Christian life which he is concerned about is possible only as a gift of God. Intercessory prayer is the explicit recognition that the "blessing" prayed for can only be given by God. It is also an act of faith in God as the one who wants to give.

As previously in this letter (1:3,17), Paul addresses his prayer not to Christ but to the Father. This corresponds to his view of salvation which originates in the Father and is communicated to men through Christ in the Spirit (1:13-14).

Even while praying, however, Paul does not miss the opportunity to convey his understanding of the gospel. *Lex orandi, lex credendi* is a principle verified supremely in Paul. Here he describes the Father as the one "from whom every family in heaven and earth is named" (v.15). We have seen how, from the very beginning of this letter, Paul has been preoccupied with the idea of unity. In particular, he has suggested that it is not Abraham who is the universal Father but God (1:4). This is the point which he stresses now. Through the Christ event (1:18), all men, indeed all creatures, have one common Father. According to Paul, it is this fact that establishes the basis of the human community and of man's harmony with the rest of the universe. What is more, it is this same Father who has "named", that is created every family. In asking God for what follows, Paul is doing no more than requesting him to carry out his own plan which he has conceived as a loving Father. Such a prayer makes sense only as an attempt to change Paul and his readers to welcome this plan. It can in no way affect God himself.

Paul's prayer is that his readers should *become* what they already *are* in virtue of the Christ-event (vv.16-19). As the church, they are already "the fulness of him who fills all in all" (1:23). And yet Paul prays here that they "may be filled with all the fulness of God" (3:19). To achieve this veritable end of salvation, the readers must allow themselves to be thoroughly renovated by God's Spirit, that is to lead his life. In other words, they must let Christ live in their hearts. Here, again, is the "Trinity": Father (v.14), Spirit (v.16), Christ (v.17). Christ dwells in men's hearts by faith. Thus faith is here something quite different from an assent of the mind. It is clearly the submission of one's whole life to the Other that is God as he has revealed himself in Christ. Basically God has revealed himself as love (1:5) and it is only if we are "rooted and grounded in love" that we will be able to understand God's wisdom (3:10). Such an understanding is a matter not of the mind but of the heart. Probably referring to the Gnostics in the community, Paul emphasises that the proper Christian knowledge of "gnosis" is the love of Christ, that is the love which God has revealed in and through Christ (v.19). It is this love that is the unique motivation of the Christian. If a person really "knows" this love in the biblical sense of having direct experience of it, of actually loving with Christ's love, then he cannot but be "filled with the fulness of God" who is love.

EXCURSUS:
The Gospel, Faith.

The Gospel

WE HAVE SEEN THAT, according to Paul, salvation has two sides: the "divine", that is the Father, the Son and the Spirit, and the "creaturely", that is the created universe, particularly man. There is obviously no clear separation, let alone a chasm, between these two sides, since, on the one hand, the very terms by which the "divine" is designated are relative or relational – they refer to creation itself. On the other hand, the created universe is directed towards the "divine" by the very roots of its being: we were "chosen" "before the foundation of the world" (1:4) and the recapitulation of the universe is the Father's "plan for the fulness of time" (1:10). For Paul God does not exist without his creation.

Nevertheless, there is, according to Paul, a necessary link between the "divine" and the creature and this is the "gospel". Perhaps we should say rather that it is the "gospel" that establishes the salvific relationship between creation and God. For it is the "gospel" that contains and reveals God's saving plan. It is the means whereby this plan is presented and communicated to man, even the condition under which the Spirit operates. Without the "gospel" man would not know of this plan and, therefore, would be radically unable to accept it. Indeed, without the "gospel" there would be no plan and, therefore, no salvation at all.

As we have seen, an essential condition of salvation is that is must be received. But unless it is presented, literally, in an acceptable form it obviously cannot be received.

To understand the vital importance of the "gospel" in Paul's scheme of things, it is necessary to realize that, according to him, salvation is communicated, and is accessible, to man only in word, that is by revelation. In reflecting on his notion of God, we saw that God is a revealing God, one who manifests his love for his creation. This entails that, to be saved, man must have this love presented to him and receive it. God's salvation is not an external reality which God applies to man "from outside". It is essentially a spiritual, interior condition of being, involving man's radical conversion and transformation. It is nothing more or less that a participation in God's own life. God's so-called saving acts in Christ – especially Christ's death and resurrection – do not effect man in any automatic, let alone "magical", sense. They are of no use to any one who has not heard them. And this "hearing" is not just *about* Christ; it is the hearing *of Christ*, that is of the meaning of Christ. What is more, the reality of salvation is not separable from the revelation and, therefore, the acceptance of this reality. Revelation is an integral part of salvation itself. Now, if God's saving plan is the revelation of his love, the "gospel" is the revelation of this plan. It spells the plan out in human terms.

The "gospel" (1:13; 3:6,7; 6,15,19), along with the apostolic ministry and preaching, which are at its service (3:1-13; 6:19-20), is not accessory to salvation but an integral part of it. The "gospel" is not just *about* Christ, it represents Christ, in the strict sense of this term, that is it renders him present. Preaching is itself the Christ-event for each generation of believers who hear the "gospel". The "gospel" is "the word of truth" (1:13), in the biblical sense of "word", that is an effective power which accomplishes precisely what it signifies (Is 55:10-17). Only – and this needs to be re-emphasized – it does this only *as* word. It is only because, and in so far as, it is heard that it achieves its purpose.

This "dynamic" view of the "gospel" enables Paul to present it as the instrumental cause of salvation: it is *through* the gospel that we have become "partakers of the promise in Christ Jesus" (3:6), just as it is by having heard it that we "were sealed with the promised Holy Spirit" (1:13). The word "gospel" means "good news" and it is possibly a term which Paul himself has forged in order to convey his understanding of the Christ-event. For him this is an essentially happy event, being the accomplishment of the Father's loving plan for his universe (1:10) and his gift to men of "the unsearchable riches of Christ" (3:8). But this event is also "news": it needs to be announced. Knowledge of it cannot be acquired by human enquiry. The preaching of the "gospel" is itself a "grace" (3:2,8). Thus, although, in the order of being, it appears to come last in God's saving plan: this plan, realized in Christ's death and resurrection, is *then* preached to all men, in fact it comes first in the order of our knowledge. We know of God's saving plan only in and through the "gospel". Without the "gospel" we would remain in ignorance of our true destiny as God's children. This "gospel" does not only reveal God's plan to us: many good plans have been shelved. Most importantly, it announces that this plan has been carried out in Christ. And it is because it has been realized in *this man* Jesus that it is essentially "goods news" for all other men. The word "good", however, indicates a perceived value. Man can appreciate the "Jesus story" as "good" only in so far as it corresponds to his innate, God-given desires, hopes and aspirations. The "gospel" is the announcement that all these have been realized in Jesus and that this fulfilment is available to all other men, provided only that they will accept it by faith.

Faith

On God's side salvation involves his plan to make men his children and to re-unite the whole universe through and in Christ and by the Spirit. This is what we might call the "objective" aspect of salvation. This plan is revealed as accomplished through the "gospel". The "gospel" is the revelation both of the details of God's saving plan and of the fact that this plan has been realized through Christ. It is in the "gospel" that salvation is made real and accessible to men. But the "gospel" is "word" and, therefore, of its very nature, must be heard, received and understood in order to be effective. Men are saved only if, and in so far as, they hear, receive and understand the "gospel". It is this complex activity that Paul calls "faith" or "believing". And it is what we might describe as the subjective aspect of salvation, that is man's role in salvation.

For Paul faith is not the mere assent of the mind to an abstract truth revealed by God. It does indeed have an intellectual or "noetic" aspect, in so far as it concerns God's plan. But the truth involved in God's plan is, quite literally, a vital or life-giving truth. It is the truth that God wants and has made it possible for all men to be his children. The attitude corresponding to such truth is more than an assent of the mind. It is an attitude of being, whereby man opens himself to the "gospel" and allows this "word" to become effective within him, that is to achieve what it signifies. In the "gospel" God tells men that they are his children. By faith they actually become his children. Without faith divine filiation is impossible.

Thus faith is the necessary human counterpart to God's revelation. From what we have seen about the role of the Spirit, there is obviously a very close connection between the activity of the Spirit and faith. It is by faith that a man is susceptible to the Spirit. Paul is very explicit on this point in Ephesians: ". . . . .and having believed in him (that is, Christ), were sealed with the promised Holy Spirit" (1:13). According to Paul, therefore, faith is the point of contact between God and man, the opening through which God gains access to man. Faith is a means of salvation: "For by grace you have been saved *through* faith" (2:8). It is the necessary condition for the working of God's saving power: ". . . . .and what is the immeasurable greatness of his power in us *who believe*" (1:19), just as it is *through* faith that Christ dwells in our hearts (3:17). Thus faith is not only man's response to salvation, it is an integral part of salvation itself. For without faith there is no salvation, men cannot be saved.

Faith also includes a strong element of trust and confidence in God who, in the act of faith, is recognized as reliable and completely willing and able to accomplish his plan within man. Paul undoubtedly sees Chrst's self-abandoning death as the expression and revelation of this aspect of faith (5:2). It is in fact very important to realize that it is only *in Christ* that faith is possible. This phrase: "in Christ", is ambiguous in English. It can mean either that Christ is the object of faith or that he is the means, the instrument, the medium of faith. In the original Greek the sense is much clearer. When Paul refers to his readers as "the saints who are also *faithful in Christ Jesus*" (1:1), he does not mean merely that Christ is the object of their faith, but that he is the means whereby they believe, the condition of their faith. It is only *in* Christ that they can believe, just as it is only *in* Christ that they are saved. Their faith is a communication in the very faith of Christ himself. The phrase "in him" in 1:13 has the same meaning. Thus faith, for Paul, is a saving act possible only in Christ.

Precisely because faith is possible only *in* Christ, it is, in reality God's activity within man. Although it is totally man's attitude towards God's saving plan, it is also totally "divine", in so far as it is God's work within man: "For by grace you have been saved through faith; and this is not your own doing, it is the gift of God" (2:7). Faith is the vehicle of God's grace, the God-given means by which man becomes a beneficiary of salvation. It is itself a grace, that is a perfectly free gift. Unless a man benefits from this gift he cannot see, hear, recognize and welcome God's saving plan in his regard. Thus God does not only save man, he also, in saving him, gives him the ability to accept this salvation. It is in faith that the admirable union between man and God, which is the essence of salvation, is achieved. Faith is both the means to this salvation and its end. Thus the state of salvation can be called one of "faith" (4:5) which is itself susceptible of development, growth and maturation (4:13).

According to Paul, faith is a paradox. On the one hand, it means the complete surrender and abandonment of self and of selfish attitudes and values, in favour of sole filial reliance on the "other" that is God revealing himself to us in Christ. But, on the other hand, it is precisely through this "way of the cross" that we achieve true selfhood, that is our real identity as God's children. In fact the profound meaning of divine sonship has been revealed to us in Christ's death and resurrection. It is only by faith, which is a real death to self and a living to the Father, that we participate in the "mystery" of Christ's death and resurrection and so become the Father's children *in* him. Our baptism, which is the ritual "plunging" into Christ's death leading to our "rising" with him, is the symbolic expression or "sacrament" of this faith. Sacrament and faith are two sides of the same coin, and both characterize the Christian life as a permanent condition of dying and rising with Christ.

Doxology.
3:20-21.

20Now to him who by the power at work within us is able to do far more abundantly than all that we ask or think, 21to him be glory in the church and in Christ Jesus to all generations, for ever and ever. Amen.

Paul ends the first part of his letter, as he began it (1:3-14), with a prayer of praise. Here it is in the form of a doxology. Paul expresses what has been implicit in all his intercessory prayers: the achievement of our salvation is the execution of God's own plan. It is his work within us. Thus there can really be no question of our informing God of our needs in this regard. The most that we can do is to remove the obstacles to his work within us, and the best way to do this is to acknowledge explicitly and formally that he is the supreme influence in our lives. As we have seen (1:6), such recognition is more than a matter of words. It is ultimately a question of a new way of life which corresponds to the revelation which God has made of his "glory". According to Paul, this renewal is possible only in the church which is Christ's body.

EXHORTATION.
4:1-6:20.

IN THE FIRST PART of his "homily" (1:3-3:21) Paul has concentrated on what could be called the "objective" aspect of our salvation, that is on what God has done for us in Christ. The very literary form in which he has done this: prayer, has served to bring out God's initiative in this salvation. In the second part of this "homily" (4:1-6:20) Paul turns to the "subjective" aspect of our salvation, that is to what we have to do to be saved. It is important to note, however, that Paul does not consider man's salvation to be a matter of co-operation between man and God, in the sense that both man and God contribute to it. According to Paul it is *totally* the work of God. Certainly man has to receive salvation by faith, but this faith is itself God's gift, communicated in Christ (1:1). In the present section of his "homily" Paul will indeed exhort his readers to right moral behaviour, but he has already told them that "we are his workmanship, created in Christ Jesus for good works, which God prepared beforehand, that we should walk in them" (2:10). Even, indeed especially, our "good works" are really God's work within us. Believing means allowing God to do this work within us.

The whole of our moral life is also a "grace" in so far as it depends upon the apostolic exhortation. Just as we would not know of God's saving plan – and, therefore, could not be properly "saved" – without the preaching of the gospel, so we would not know how to behave without the apostolic exhortation. Without this latter, the gospel might easily be perverted into a new kind of "gnosis" in which knowledge is stressed to the exclusion of action. According to Paul, God's wisdom itself is supremely active. It concerns man's salvation. In the final analysis, it is identifiable with his love. It is not surprising, therefore, that man's participation in this wisdom should go beyond mere knowledge and include love. The profound significance of the whole of this section of our letter is summed up in the old Latin tag: *agere sequitur esse* – "activity follows existence". If a man really *is* a Christian he will *act* in a certain way. But both his new existence and his new behaviour are a "grace".

EXCURSUS: CHRISTIAN BEHAVIOUR.

FOR PAUL salvation is primarily a question of being: through our reception of the "gospel", by faith, we have become God's children, we *are* holy. Nevertheless, throughout the second main part of Ephesians, Paul exhorts his readers to behave in a manner which corresponds to this ontological status.

The simple fact that Paul *exhorts* his readers has certain implications. To begin with, it implies that the morality appropriate to the "gospel" is not "automatic". Proper acceptance of the "gospel" is not a mere assent of the mind to an abstract, external truth. It is the welcome given to God's effective word, which always produces what it signifies. But this word will not bear fruit unless the person receiving it actually and personally behaves accordingly. This behaviour is both totally human, in so far as it is really the individual person who is acting, and totally "divine", in so far as it is the expression of God's word working profoundly and discretely within the believer. This word does not merely respect man's pre-existing or innate freedom. Rather, it makes him free, in so far as it reveals to him new possibilities for his existence and enables him to realize these possibilities. But Paul's exhortation refers more to the "personal" aspect of this behaviour, to man's ability (always *in* Christ) to "appropriate" God's word. Thus exhortation supposes the possibility of a man refusing to behave according to the "gospel". From what we have seen, it is obvious that such a man would not even receive the gospel. Christian morality is not subsequent to Christian faith. It is implied within the faith. There is no Christian faith which is not active or acted faith.

The apostolic exhortation focuses attention on this personally active aspect of salvation. It is worthwhile noting that a half of Ephesians is dedicated to it, while the other half (ostensibly the "dogmatic" or "doctrinal" part) is given to a description of God's work in and for us. Even this latter part is really the basis of the exhortation: "I *therefore* . . . beg you" (4:1). Paul's main aim in Ephesians is a pastoral one: to get his readers to lead the Christian life. His central thesis is that the "gospel", of its very nature, demands a certain kind of behaviour. Without this behaviour, those who might call themselves "Christian" have not even begun to believe. Thus exhortation is a function of Paul's apostolate. It is not accessory to his preaching, but an integral part of it, in so far as it corresponds to the nature of his "gospel" itself.

Concentration on the active or acted aspect of salvation also shows that the Christian reality is at the antipodes of Gnosticism, for which salvation was merely a matter of the mind, enlightened by "gnosis", that is knowledge. Such a view of salvation obviously had little if any regard for a morality which involved the stuff of every day life. Now Paul makes it abundantly clear that the knowledge and truth communicated in the "gospel" necessitates a change and transformation of the whole human person, body and soul, matter and spirit (4:20-24), as an individual and as a member of society.

What we can gather already from the form of Paul's exhortation, is confirmed by the content of the "gospel" itself. This "gospel" is the good news that God has accomplished his plan to make men his children and to unify the universe in Christ. It is obvious that, as far as men are concerned, if this plan is to be *real* for them, that is if they are actually and personally to be God's children, to enjoy the divine life, then they must "realize" this plan within themselves and *be* what they *are*, and behave as such. This observation is not as tautologous as it may appear at first sight. We have seen that, according to Paul, salvation is both objective and subjective. It is only achieved when God's "objective" holiness and the Spirit of sonship are received and appropriated subjectively and personally by men. We need to maintain that even this subjective appropriation is a "grace", God's work within men, but it is still personal for all that – indeed precisely because of that. According to Paul, this personal aspect of salvation implies morality. It could be said that, for Paul, morality is the whole purpose, the "incorporation" of the "gospel".

We have seen that holiness and divine sonship are objective realities, given to men by God. They are not acquired by human effort. But they are both what we might call "relational" or relative realities, that is they refer to other realities or imply other things. God's holiness does indeed mean his transcendence, the fact that he is beyond or different from his creatures. But, ironically, this "difference" is revealed in the Bible (and supremely in Christ) to reside in the fact that God wishes to communicate with his creatures. His apartness turns out to be his communicability; his aloneness is revealed as his desire to be with others and for others to be with him. His unique self-possession is his will to give and to share. In other words, his holiness is, in the final analysis, his love, his concern for his creatures. That by which he is "different" is the very characteristic by which he is one with others. Now if men share in this holiness, it is obvious that they must also be "extra-vert". If they are caught up in God's holiness they must not only be *like* God, they must also *be* God in the sense that they are the channels and the vehicles of God's love. Because they are holy with God's holiness they must not be apart from anything. On the contrary, they must be one with creation, they must give to, and communicate with others. And all this is the actualization in their own lives of the one holiness of God. Christian holiness does not involve a separation from the world, except where this term can be understood in a pejorative sense, as that which is necessarily evil (4:22). It implies a commitment, a mission to the world. Christian holiness is necessarily consecration. In other words, being holy means sharing in God's concern for his creation. It is precisely through men, living within the ordinary social structures of this world, that God's loving concern is realized.

Being a son means being related with the other person who is father. In the Bible sonship is characterized particularly by obedience. If we have the Spirit of sonship, if we really *are* God's children we will be united with him in his concern for his creation. We will want precisely what he wants. Our divine sonship is not only a guarantee of our final inheritance (1:14), it is also a commission to represent the Father in the world.

Thus when we consider either our holiness or our divine sonship in Christ we can see why for Paul a new kind of behaviour, "good works" (2:10), flows from, and is demanded by, the "truth" that is the "gospel" (4:21). In 4:15 the R.S.V. reads: "Rather, *speaking the truth* in love, we are to grow up in every way into him who is the head, into Christ". The preceding verse (4:14) does not call for the contrast "speaking the truth". And in fact the original Greek has: "*being truthful* . . . . ." This makes better sense. It is precisely in *being* "truthful", that is by living according to the "truth" that is in Jesus (4:21) that we achieve salvation. Truth for Paul is not only what we *believe*, it is what we *do*. And it is by *doing* the truth that we *are* holy and God's children. Finally for Paul there is no conflict between being and activity. Because God, the supreme Being, has revealed himself in Christ as supremely active and powerful.

Paul stresses that these "good works" are the effect of God's work within the believer: "For we are his workmanship, created in Christ Jesus for good works, which God prepared beforehand that we should walk in them" (2:10). In Christ God has showed us precisely how to behave. It is by behaving accordingly that we are created in Christ and achieve our proper destiny.

Exhortation To All Believers.
4:1-5:20.

The "blessing" which opened this work (1:3-14) provides the key to the correct understanding of Paul's view of Christian morality. Just as this prayer is essentially responsive, being impossible without the revelation of the Mystery (1:9), so the new life of the Christian is essentially responsive and impossible without the interior action of God within the believer. Nevertheless, this new morality requires an effort, an effort which is the expression in man of God's power. Paul connects both parts of his work with a succinct "therefore" (v.1). There is no contrast in his mind between prayer and action. A proper understanding of the "mystery" must entail a new moral life, just as the summit of this new life is the explicit and formal "blessing" of God. Significantly, the object of Paul's first exhortation is unity within the Church (vv.2-16). This unity is presented as the practical realisation of the unity which has been achieved by Christ. It is not uniformity but the unity of a body to which the Church is again compared.

UNITY.
4:1-16.

4 I therefore, a prisoner for the Lord, beg you to lead a life worthy of the calling to which you have been called, 2with all lowliness and meekness, with patience, forbearing one another in love, 3eager to maintain the unity of the Spirit in the bond of peace. 4There is one body and one Spirit, just as you were called to the one hope that belongs to your call, 5one Lord, one faith, one baptism, 6one God and Father of us all, who is above all and through all and in all. 7But grace was given to each of us according to the measure of Christ's gift. 8Therefore it is said,

"When he ascended on high he led a host of captives, and he gave gifts to men."

9(In saying, "He ascended," what does it mean but that he had also descended into the lower parts of the earth? 10He who descended is he who also ascended far above all the heavens, that he might fill all things.) 11And his gifts were that some should be apostles, some prophets, some evangelists, some pastors and teachers, 12for the equipment of the saints, for the work of ministry, for building up the body of Christ, 13until we all attain to the unity of the faith and of the knowledge of the Son of God, to mature manhood, to the measure of the stature of the fullness of Christ; [14]so that we may no longer be children, tossed to and fro and carried about with every wind of doctrine, by the cunning of men, by their craftiness in deceitful wiles. [15]Rather, speaking the truth in love, we are to grow up in every way into him who is the head, into Christ, [16]from whom the whole body, joined and knit together by every joint with which it is supplied, when each part is working properly, makes bodily growth and upbuilds itself in love.

Paul's first exhortation is addressed to all believers, regardless of their social condition. He describes himself as "a prisoner for the Lord" as if to stress that to extort is just as much part of his apostolic role as is preaching (3:8) and praying (1:3,15; 3:1,14). This exhortation, like the gospel and prayer, is part of the Christ-event itself.

Remember that this "homily" is probably being addressed to Christians who have just been baptised. (There is a sense in which this applies to *all* Christians). All Christians have been called by God in the Word that is Christ. By being baptised they have acknowledged this call. But now they must lead a life which corresponds to it. They must answer God not only in words and by conforming to the church's baptismal ritual but also by an entirely new way of life. They must *behave* as they *are* (2:1-22). In other words, they must allow the Word that is Christ to be effective within them.

Paul's insistence on the term "call" is not without significance here. The Greek word for "church" – *ekklesia* – is a cognate of "to call". It means "the assembly or congregation of those who are called". According to Paul the church is established by God's call, addressed to all in Christ. In so far as they answer this call with a life that really corresponds to Christ they become the church. The only life worthy of this call is the life of Christ.

The sort of behaviour which Paul considers to be worthy of our call is, first and foremost, that which makes for peace and harmony within the community (vv.2-3). If all the members of the community are striving to serve one another, then there will be no danger of the unity which is of the essence of salvation (2:18) being broken. The "ontological" unity is endorsed by the "moral" harmony within the community. Clearly Paul has in mind here the local church.

In order to stress that orderly, harmonious and peaceful behaviour is the most appropriate for the Christian, Paul reminds his readers of the unity which characterises God's saving plan (vv.4-6). All men and women are called to belong to one body, enlivened by one Spirit. The unity of all nations, races and cultures could hardly be expressed more clearly. This unity is achieved by the recognition of one Lord, expressed in one baptism. The ultimate source of this unity is the oneness of God himself who, far from living in "splendid isolation", is "Father of us all". We can hardly miss Paul's "Trinity" here: "Spirit", "Lord" (Jesus Christ), "Father".

The fundamental unity of salvation, however, does not exclude a certain diversity within the church. Each and every member of the church has received a particular gift or grace from Christ (vv.7-8). This is a theme which Paul has already developed in 1 Cor 12-14 and Rom 12:3-8. There is no incompatibility between unity and diversity within the church. Indeed, true unity (as distinct from uniformity) requires diversity. It is the harmonisation of different factors and functions.

Paul here applies the imagery of Ps 68:18 to the Christ-event, finding in the two terms "ascended on high" and "gave gifts" all he needs to justify his view scripturally (v.9). He also takes this occasion to remind his readers of the saving significance of Christ's ascension: the filling of the universe with his presence, the establishment of the "pleroma" (1:23).

Paul singles out those gifts which are closely associated with preaching and teaching (v.11). His aim is to stress that these functions within the church are ordained by

Christ. They are not subsequent to the Christ-event but part of it. These gifts are for the benefit, and at the service, of the whole church, "the saints", to enable all the members of the church to exercise a ministry. This universal or common ministry has only one purpose: the edification of Christ's body (v.12). Paul here mixes two metaphors: that of the building (2:20-22) and that of the body (1:23), with the effect of suggesting that the final accomplishment of God's plan for the universe will be achieved through the members of the church. In fact this plan is still far from being completed. We are still moving towards unity and maturity. It is only when all are united in faith and in the knowledge of the Son of God that they will be fully mature and, by that very fact, Christ will have accomplished his mission (v.13).

Being mature means having left behind the fickleness and vulnerability of childhood (v.14). More positively, it means being in perfect unison with Christ our head and the other members of his body (v.15). The principle of this harmony is love. This is the vital source running throughout the whole body and binding the members, ligaments and joints together (v.16). Of all the places where Paul uses the metaphor of the body (1 Cor 12:12-31; Rom 12:4-8) this is the one where he exploits it to the full. It seems impossible to envisage a more profound unity between Christ and his church, on the one hand, and other men and women among themselves, on the other, than that which pertains between the different members of a body. This is the unity towards which Paul's readers must strive.

NEW MORAL BEHAVIOUR.
4:17-5:20.

In a fairly long section (4:17-5:20) Paul describes the radical conversion which is required of those who have been re-created in Christ. This passage is enough to exonerate Paul of any suspicion of gnosticism, for all his insistence on "knowledge" in the first main part of his letter. He is quite specific in the demands which he makes on the "saints". This exhortation, too, corresponds exactly to Paul's view of the "mystery". If Christ, by his death, has created in himself one new man (2:15), the Christian, in accepting this work of Christ, must "put on" this new man by a new moral behaviour (4:22-24). The mention of "putting off" and "putting on" is doubtless a reference to the baptismal ceremony which is clearly in the background to Ephesians. Because the Christian has been re-created or re-generated in baptism the essence of his new behaviour consists in nothing more or less than the imitation of God himself (4:32-5:2).

[17]Now this I affirm and testify in the Lord, that you must no longer live as the Gentiles do, in the futility of their minds; [18]they are darkened in their understanding, alienated from the life of God because of the ignorance that is in them, due to their hardness of heart; [19]they have become callous and have given themselves up to licentiousness, greedy to practice every kind of uncleanness. [20]You did not so learn Christ!—[21]assuming that you have heard about him and were taught in him, as the truth is in Jesus. [22]Put off your old nature which belongs to your former manner of life and is corrupt through deceitful lusts, [23]and be renewed in the spirit of your minds, [24]and put on the new nature, created after the likeness of God in true righteousness and holiness.

[25]Therefore, putting away falsehood, let every one speak the truth with his neighbor, for we are members one of another. [26]Be angry but do not sin; do not let the sun go down on your anger, [27]and give no opportunity to the devil. [28]Let the thief no longer steal, but rather let him labor, doing honest work with his hands, so that he may be able to give to those in need. [29]Let no evil talk come out of your mouths, but only such as is good for edifying, as fits the occasion, that it may impart grace

to those who hear. [30]And do not grieve the Holy Spirit of God, in whom you were sealed for the day of redemption. [31]Let all bitterness and wrath and anger and clamor and slander be put away from you, with all malice, [32]and be kind to one another, tenderhearted, forgiving one another, as God in Christ forgave you.

5   Therefore be imitators of God, as beloved children. [2]And walk in love, as Christ loved us and gave himself up for us, a fragrant offering and sacrifice to God.

[3]But immorality and all impurity or covetousness must not even be named among you, as is fitting among saints. [4]Let there be no filthiness, nor silly talk, nor levity, which are not fitting; but instead let there be thanksgiving. [5]Be sure of this, that no immoral or impure man, or one who is covetous (that is, an idolator), has any inheritance in the kingdom of Christ and of God. [6]Let no one deceive you with empty words, for it is because of these things that the wrath of God comes upon the sons of disobedience. [7]Therefore do not associate with them, [8]for once you were darkness, but now you are light in the Lord; walk as children of light [9](for the fruit of light is found in all that is good and right and true), [10]and try to learn what is pleasing to the Lord. [11]Take no part in the unfruitful works of darkness, but instead expose them. [12]For it is a shame even to speak of the things that they do in secret; [13]but when anything is exposed by the light it becomes visible, for anything that becomes visible is light. [14]Therefore it is said,

"Awake, O sleeper, and arise from the dead,
and Christ shall give you light."

[15]Look carefully then how you walk, not as unwise men but as wise, [16]making the most of the time, because the days are evil. [17]Therefore do not be foolish, but understand what the will of the Lord is. [18]And do not get drunk with wine, for that is debauchery; but be filled with the Spirit, [19]addressing one another in psalms and hymns and spiritual songs, singing and making

melody to the Lord with all your heart, [20]always and for everything giving thanks in the name of our Lord Jesus Christ to God the Father.

You Did Not So Learn Christ!
4:17-21.

If Christians must work positively towards the construction of Christ's body, negatively they must desist from their previous Gentile behaviour. Obviously Paul is here (v.17) referring particularly to those of Gentile origin. In 2:1-10 he described how they had been rescued "objectively" from their hopeless plight. Now he exhorts them to ratify and endorse this redemption. As in Romans 1:18-32, Paul here considers what we would normally regard as sin: callousness, licentiousness, impurity, not so much as sin itself as the symptom or the effect of the only "real" sin: hardness of heart giving rise to a culpable ignorance (vv.18-19). Paul sees the root cause of mankind's malady as a profound refusal to recognise and acknowledge the truth. This is doubtless because he is convinced and God has saved the universe by revealing the truth that is Christ (1:9). This truth is addressed not merely to our minds – we learn *Christ* not *about* him! – but also to our whole person. It is a living, life-giving, transforming truth, liberating us from our self-destructive behaviour (vv.20-21).

Put On The New Nature.
4:22-32.

In 2:15 Paul has referred to Christ's "creation" of the new man. Now (vv.22-24) he exhorts his readers to divest themselves of their old nature (lit: "man") and put on the new nature (lit: "man"). This "new man" is none other than Christ himself *in* whom we have been re-created. Here Paul uses another metaphor: that of clothing. The particular value of this metaphor is that it expresses *our* participation in the work of our salvation: we really do change our whole way of life. There is a real renewal in our minds. This conversion is symbolised by the changing of clothes connected with baptism. Paul is probably referring to this practice, while intimating that what is being changed is not so much a garment as a whole way of life. It is when we "put on" Christ in this way that we achieve our true destiny as the image of God (Gen 1:26).

Paul does not content himself with a general exhortation to an interior renewal, however profound. Here (vv.25-32) he becomes quite specific and concentrates on those areas of morality which concern personal relationships. The motivation for this social morality is very clear: membership of the one body (v.25), presence of the Holy Spirit (v.30), the example of God himself (v.32). According to Paul, the Christian's status as a child of God demands that he behaves as such.

Be Imitators of God.
5:1-2.

The "new man" is created in the image and likeness of God (4:23). It follows that the new manner of life appropriate to the Christian is nothing more or less than the imitation of God. If the whole of God's saving work can be resumed in the one notion of divine filiation (1:5), the whole of Christian morality can be summed up in that of divine imitation. If the Christian wants to know how he or she should behave he has only to contemplate the way in which God has behaved towards his creation. As if the love of God himself were not sufficient a guide (1:6), Paul proposes the loving example of Christ. We are called (4:1) to love one another as Christ has loved us (Jn 13:34). And there is no mistaking the nature of this love: it is self-giving service to the point of death. For the Christian loving is giving, and forgiving (4:32). This is the sort of love which Paul has been talking about since 4:2. It is the only recipe for a peaceful, harmonious community.

Such love is also the only worship worthy of God. Christ offered a sacrifice to God, in dying for us. God was glorified in service rendered to mankind. Similarly, we worship God by serving our fellows. This is not just *a* form of worship among several others. It is the *only* form suitable for a God who *is* Father, that is who is himself totally "for" the others who are his children.

Walk as Children of Light.
5:3-20.

We have already seen (1:1) that, for Paul, holiness is not primarily good moral behaviour. It is the state of being in which we are placed at our baptism. Nevertheless, as Paul makes clear here (vv.3-6), there are some kinds of behaviour which are not compatible with holiness. How we behave really does effect our relationship with God. This point may seem fairly obvious to us today, but Paul clearly saw the need to emphasise it. It would even appear that some people were teaching that Christians were in some way exonerated from moral obligations (1 Cor 10:23). Referring to the moral dualism which we have seen previously (2:2,3), Paul insists that there is a behaviour which displeases God.

By their conversion and baptism Christians are separated from the "sons of disobedience" (2:2,3) as light is separated from darkness (vv.7-8). Now, therefore, they must behave like the children of light and produce what is "good and right and true". All that the Christian is separated from is the evil in the world, not from the world itself. Even with regard to this evil, the Christian's attitude should not be one of mere flight. He should expose the evils in the world by projecting his light upon them, that is by leading his new life in the world (v.11-13). Because Paul's dualism is not metaphysical but moral, neither is it radically pessimistic. He envisages the conversion of the "sons of disobedience", the illumination of the sons of darkness, precisely through the obedience and the "light" of the Christians. After all, as Paul reminds us (quoting an early Christian hymn), we were once asleep, dead and in darkness, but Christ has given us light and new life (v.14). This light is not just for ourselves. We are the light of the world (Mt 5:14-16). We are the means, the reflectors, by which Christ, *the* light of the world (Jn 9:5), is continually projected on the world. The sectaries of Qumran considered themselves to be the "sons of light" opposed to the "sons of darkness" but they had no awareness of a mission to the world. According to Paul, however, the church is essentially missionary (1 Cor 14:22-25).

We have seen (1:10) that, according to Paul, the "fulness of time" has arrived in one sense while, in another, it is still to come. For the moment the church is still waiting for the final accomplishment of God's saving plan which – given that the most important phase has passed – cannot be far off. During the intervening period, however, the church is not to wait passively for the end. It must "make the most of the time", precisely by considering carefully the way it behaves. In the circumstances in which the church finds itself, this is obviously the only "wise" course of action (vv.15-17).

All through the present section of his "homily" Paul has called for what we would consider integrity: the precise conformity between the "subjective" and the "objective" aspects of our salvation. This applies even to the Spirit. By our baptism we do in fact already have the Spirit (1:13; 2:18; 4:3,4). But Paul now exhorts us to be *filled* with the Spirit. This can only mean that we should allow the Spirit to be fully active in our lives. In v.18 Paul verges on the comical and we are reminded of Luke's description of the first Pentecost (Acts 2:12,15f.). More importantly, Paul expresses his conviction that it is the Spirit that is the source and inspiration of prayer in the church (Rom 8:26-27). Paul singles out the prayer of thanksgiving (of which he has already given us an example, 1:15f.). This prayer is essentially "Trinitarian": it is addressed *to* God the Father, *in the name of* our Lord Jesus Christ, *in* the Spirit (v.20). Because it is in the Spirit, it is not confined to either time or place. Nor is it restricted to only some things. It is universal thanksgiving, for everything.

Exhortation to Particular Categories of Believers. 5:21-6:9.

It is the precise relationship between the Church and Christ, which provides the basis for Paul's next exhortation; to wives and husbands (5:21-33). The new relationship between wife and husband is to be modelled on the relationship between the Church and Christ. This exhortation enables Paul to express yet another image of the Church. Previously in Ephesians he has presented the Church as Christ's body (1:23; 4:16) and a holy temple (2:21). Now he sees it as a bride, thus emphasising the eminently personal relationship between the Church and Christ.

The exhortation to wives and husbands not unnaturally leads to the exhortation to children and parents (6:1-4). Paul considers that a true grasp of the "mystery", far from being merely a matter of the intellect, affects the whole of man's personal, social and family life.

The "family" included slaves in Paul's day. It is natural, therefore, that he should see the Christ-event as impinging on the slave-master relationship (5:5-9).

> [21]Be subject to one another out of reverence for Christ. [22]Wives, be subject to your husbands, as to the Lord. [23]For the husband is the head of the wife as Christ is the head of the church, his body, and is himself its Savior. [24]As the church is subject to Christ, so let wives also be subject in everything to their husbands. [25]Husbands, love your wives, as Christ loved the church and gave himself up for her, [26]that he might sanctify her, having cleansed her by the washing of water with the word,

27that the church might be presented before him in splendor, without spot or wrinkle or any such thing, that she might be holy and without blemish. 28Even so husbands should love their wives as their own bodies. He who loves his wife loves himself. 29For no man ever hates his own flesh, but nourishes and cherishes it, as Christ does the church, 30because we are members of his body. 31"For this reason man shall leave his father and mother and be joined to his wife, and the two shall become one." 32This is a great mystery, and I take it to mean Christ and the church; 33however, let each one of you love his wife as himself, and let the wife see that she respects her husband.

6   Children, obey your parents in the Lord, for this is right. 2"Honor your father and mother" (this is the first commandment with a promise), 3"that it may be well with you and that you may live long on the earth." 4Fathers, do not provoke your children to anger, but bring them up in the discipline and instruction of the Lord.

5Slaves, be obedient to those who are your earthly masters, with fear and trembling, in singleness of heart, as to Christ; 6not in the way of eye-service, as men-pleasers, but as servants of Christ, doing the will of God from the heart, rendering service with a good will as to the Lord and not to men, 8knowing that whatever good any one does, he will receive the same again from the Lord, whether he is a slave or free. 9Masters, do the same to them, and forbear threatening, knowing that he who is both their Master and yours is in heaven, and that there is no partiality with him.

Wives and Husbands.
5:21-33.

Paul's second exhortation is addressed to believers in their different domestic situations. Just as their conversion has committed them to a way of life which is radically different from their previous one, so it obliges them to continue to lead their family life in a fundamentally new way. It is important to note at this point that Paul does not see the gospel as either introducing new institutions into society or abolishing old ones. Here, for instance, he is neither claiming that marriage is a Christian "sacrament" nor that slavery should be abolished. What he is demanding is that these human institutions should be seen now in the light of Christ, and that the faithful should behave within them as the followers of Christ. Thus he has not abandoned the principle which he enunciated in 1 Cor 7:17-24: "let everyone lead the life which the Lord has assigned to him, and in which God has called him" (v.17).

Thus Paul has a profound respect for the structures and institutions of society, just as he is radically optimistic with regard to the "world" as a whole (5:11,13). Although he is convinced that "the form of this world is passing away" (1 Cor 7:31), he does not urge his readers to neglect it in any way. His Christianity is in no way "other worldly". While the Christian is indeed waiting for the final accomplishment of salvation he must "make the most of the time" (5:16) by leading his life in this world in the spirit of Christ. At the same time, this spirit (being none other than the Spirit) has a transforming effect on social structures and institutions, making them the very instruments of salvation. In the final analysis the salvation of the universe will be seen to have been accomplished by God not from "outside" but from "within", that is through the structures of the universe itself. This, after all, is the profound significance of the "incarnation".

Be Subject to Your Husbands.
5:21-24.

Although v.21 obviously introduces Paul's exhortation to wives, it also forms a suitable conclusion to his previous exhortation to the faithful in general, especially as far as their interpersonal relationships within the church are concerned. For if their aim is to "be subject to one another", that is to serve one another, there can be no fear of disharmony and disunity within the community (4:2-6). Their only motive for this mutual service is "reverence for Christ". It is Christ who, both as the revelation of the Father's service (1:6) and as servant himself (v.2), is the unique norm of Christian behaviour. The disciple of the one who "came not to be served but to serve and to give his life as a ransom for many" (Mk 10:45) cannot but be a servant. Service is the hallmark of the Christian, whether this is within the church (4:12) or within the world (vv.11-13). It is only in serving others that we revere Christ (Matt 25:31-46).

Thus the "subjection" to which Paul exhorts wives is but one instance of the universal, mutual subjection which he would expect from all the faithful. His view of marriage, however, suggests to him that wives have a particular motivation to be "subject" to the "others" who are their husbands. This motivation is the fact that Christ is the "head" of the church. By being subject to their husbands they are realising this truth. Their domestic status is a "grace" in the sense that it is a situation in which they are continually reminded of the obligation which they have (along with all the other faithful, including their husbands) to be subject to others. Modern feminists would be wrong to resent Paul's basic message here. As we have seen, he is not introducing the institution of marriage. He accepts it as it is, but shows that those Christians who are wives have, within marriage, the opportunity to lead the Christian life of service in a special way. They are no more or no less "subject" to others than any other Christians, least of all than their husbands who are called to be "subject" to their wives by love.

Love Your Wives.
5:25-33.

The exhortation to husbands to love their wives may appear as somewhat strange, until it is realised that the love in question has nothing directly to do with sentiment, emotion or sex. It is the love neither of *eros* (sensual love) nor of *philia* (friendship) but of *agapē*, that is the attitude of self-giving, sacrificial service to which Paul has already exhorted *all* the faithful (4:2,15,16; 5:2) and which is modelled on the love which both God and Christ have shown for men (1:5,6; 2:4; 5:2). Christian love is service, yet another way of speaking about "subjection" (vv.21-24). Thus husbands are as bound to be "subjected" to their wives as wives are to "love" their husbands. Paul's pastoral concern has led him to introduce here yet another image of the church: that of the church as the bride of Christ (v.25). The idea appeared already in 2 Cor 11:2, but the present context allows him to develop it more fully. The significance of the husband-wife metaphor, following those of the body-head (1:22-23; 4:15-16; 5:23) and the temple (2:20-22), is that the relationship between the church and Christ is a personal one. Thus all these images of the church are complementary, each evincing a particular aspect or aspects of the church's nature. The body-head image brings out the supremacy of Christ, the vital union between Christ and his members, the interdependence between the different members. The temple image emphasises the church's divine and cultic character. The husband-wife image reminds us that, however profound the union between the baptised and Christ may be, it remains a free union, a relationship of persons.

Paul suggests that, if the wife-husband relationship – seen *in* Christ – can be the setting for a deeper realisation of the Christ-event (vv.22-24), the same applies to the husband-wife relationship. In the secular context of marriage the husband has the opportunity to actualise Christian love, that is Christ's love, in a particular way. Marriage for him (as indeed for his wife, in the way already seen) becomes a vocation. In this sense the secular reality is transformed, becoming the sphere in which Christ's love is, and is seen to be, effective.

There is no doubt about the kind of love Paul has in mind here. It is the love which has compelled Christ to die for the church and has made the church what it is. Such love is at the antipodes of a love based upon attractiveness in the beloved. The church is lovely precisely because Christ loves it, not *vice versa*.

The mention of cleansing by washing and the word (v.26) while possibly also reflecting bridal marriage preparations, is an obvious reference to baptism by which the church is "sanctified" (1:1).

Paul now combines the husband-wife metaphor with that of the body (vv.28-33). For the church is not only Christ's bride, in the sense of being personally distinct from him. It is also his wife in the biblical sense of being "bone of his bones and flesh of his flesh" (Gen 2:23). Reflecting on marriage has doubtless led Paul to Gen 2:24 as a good scriptural text to express the relationship between Christ and the church. We know that the Jews of New Testament times applied this text to marriage (Mt 19:5 par). In the case of man and woman, however, it obviously cannot be taken literally. Paul maintains that this "mystery", that is the profound union of the two beings mentioned in this text, is verified only of Christ and the church. But this unique relationship now sheds new light on the relationship between a man and his wife. Gen 2:24 takes on a new meaning. In Christ a man should really consider his wife as his other self.

It is worth noting that this marital love (like the wife's "subjection") is but an example of the attitude which all Christians should have towards one another. To this extent Christian marriage is not only for the respective partners. It is also a visible and tangible expression, a "sacrament", of Christ's love for the church and the world.

Children and Parents.
6:1-4.

After wives and husbands, Paul addresses children. Their duty "in the Lord" is to be obedient to their parents.

Although writing to a predominantly Gentile community, Paul does not hesitate to refer here (as indeed elsewhere in the letter) to the Jewish scriptures.

The Christian's new condition affects his attitude towards his children. He should be gentle towards them, while ensuring their education in the faith.

Slaves and Masters.
6:5-9.

After husbands, wives and children, the family also comprised slaves. Upon their conversion, their social status did not change, but their attitude ought to. Paul does not denounce the institution of slavery. As with the case of marriage, he shows that it can have a new significance in Christ. The slave should now consider that his service is addressed not to his earthly master, but to his heavenly master, Christ.

Similarly, the master should consider his position in the new light of Christ. Paul does not elaborate on the desirable attitude of the master, but simply says "do the same to them" (v.9). We can only assume that he wishes the master to have an attitude which corresponds to that of the slaves. They are to consider their service as performed for their heavenly master. He is to respect this attitude and to consider himself merely as the earthly representative of this heavenly master. It is in this way that he, too, serves the Lord. From being a master he has become a steward. If Paul does not make a full frontal attack on slavery, he is certainly here putting a time-bomb under it.

NOTE:

Love

The most striking characteristic of Paul's moral theology is that it is very specific. In exhorting his readers to lead a life worthy of ther call (4:1), he does not hesitate to give them clear examples of what he has in mind. Moreover, he shows great confidence in man's radical grasp of human values in supposing that he knows precisely what is good.

But more important is what we might call the mainspring or the guiding principle of Paul's moral theology which is love. This one notion sums up both God's revealed attitude towards his creation and, therefore, the corresponding attitude which this revelation elicits in man. Indeed in both God and man it is the same love that is in question. For there is only one true love, namely the love of God, the love that *is* God. And salvation, according to Paul, means nothing more or less than the fact that this love has been communicated to man. As he puts it in the all-important passage in Romans: "God's love has been poured into our hearts through the Holy Spirit which has been given to us" (Rom 5:5). The love referred to here is indeed God's love for us and our love for God. But it is also God's love for his creation. In giving us his love, God has made us share in his own saving love. The love with which we, as Christians, love others is God's own love. To this extent we could say that God's love for the universe is realized fully in man who, through faith and baptism, has been made the instrument or channel of this love. This certainly appears to be the implication of Paul's idea of love.

The "love" in question, that is *agapē* (as distinct from *philia*, meaning friendship, and *eros*, meaning sensuality), conveys the idea of giving, surrender, selfless consideration of others. It is a "love" which, in Paul's own words, "does not insist on its own way" (1 Cor 13:5). Thus it very fittingly describes the purely gratuitous and unwarranted "service" rendered to an inferior by a superior. It implies self-abnegating condescension, the desire to go "out" towards others. As distinct from *eros*, it is not elicited by an attractiveness in the person loved, and, as distinct from *philia*, it does not suppose a reciprocation of love. It is the love of grace or favour. It is, therefore, very appropriate as an expression of the attitude which God has evinced in the Christ-event.

In Ephesians Paul explicitly connects the Christ-event with God's love: "But God, who is rich in mercy, out of the great *love* with which he *loved* us . . . . ." (2:4); ". . . . and to know the *love* of Christ which surpasses knowledge . . ." (3:19). In the latter passage "the love of Christ" means both the love which God has revealed in Christ and Christ's own love. As we saw in reflecting on Paul's view of Christ it is precisely Christ's own attitude that reveals the attitude of his Father. Paul refers to this love in 5:2: "And walk in *love*, as Christ *loved* us and gave himself up for us, a fragrant offering and sacrifice to God", and in 5:25: "Husbands, *love* your wives, as Christ *loved* the church and gave himself up for her". Both of these passages give us an insight into Paul's idea of love. This love is here expressed in self-giving, and that to the point of death (cf. also Gal 2:20). For Paul, therefore, to love is to give utterly and completely. The model and exemplar of this love is Christ himself.

Because love is the essence of the Christ-event, it follows (especially in the light of what we have said about Paul's notion of Christian behaviour) that love is also the essence of the Christian life, that is of Christian morality. Already in his *berakah* Paul has suggested this theme. The phrase "in love" which the R.S.V. places with "he destined us" in 1:5 could be read with 1:4 to give us: "that we should be holy and blameless before him *in love*". Thus Paul could mean that Christian holiness consists precisely of love. Or perhaps the phrase is deliberately ambiguous: "in love" refers both to the way God has destined us and to the way in which we should be holy. This double meaning coincides exactly with what we have seen to be Paul's idea of holiness: it is both God's love for his creation and our participation in this love.

Certainly Paul singles out love as the most characteristic attitude of the believer. Not only does he praise it in his readers (1:15), but, more importantly, he exhorts them to love (4:2). This love is the expression and actualization of their authentic existence in Christ (4:15), the very principle of the church's growth (4:16). The new behaviour expected of them as Christians is summed up in the one exhortation: "And walk in *love*, as Christ loved us and gave himself up for us, a fragrant offering and sacrifice to God" (5:2). This love is to be exemplified particularly in the attitude of the husband towards his wife (5:25,28). But it is obviously not exclusive to husbands. Like the wife's "subjection" (5:21), it is a sign of the love which all men should have for one another (cf. 5:25). It is remarkable that Paul has to *exhort* husbands to *love* their wives. Love is usually understood to be an integral part of marriage. But the love to which Paul exhorts husbands is neither *eros* nor *philia*. It is the selfless giving and seeking the good of the other person, that is *agapē*.

The motive and inspiration of this love is God the Father himself who has shown himself as love both in Christ, his "beloved" (1:6) and in all the baptized who recognize their new dignity as his "beloved children" (5:1). God himself is the model of the new human behaviour demanded by the "gospel". Men are called to behave towards one another in exactly the same way as God has behaved towards them in Christ. True human behaviour is "divine" behaviour. In so far as God's revelation is centred on Christ, it is Christ himself who is the model and exemplar of this new behaviour. Paul tells his readers quite simply: if you want to know how to behave, just contemplate Christ.

In fact this love is the ultimate expression and realization of our participation in Christ's death and resurrection. Believing is already a kind of death and resurrection, in so far as it is an abandonment of our purely human viewpoints and a submission to God's word, which lead to a new kind of existence. But it is in love that this word (which is itself a word *of love*) has its full effect. It is by "dying" to self in the service of others, in imitation and in the power of Christ, that we actually live with him and triumph over all possible evils.

Exhortation to All the Faithful.
6:10-20.

In 1:19; 3:16 and 3:20 Paul has referred to God's power which is at work in the believer. Now he exhorts his readers to assume that power in the battle against spiritual forces (6:10-20). Significantly, the Christian's spiritual enemies are those which have already been conquered by Christ. Paul's message seems clear: God's saving plan has already been accomplished in Christ, but it has not yet been fully accomplished in his members. Christ's own triumph, however, is the guarantee that we will achieve salvation, provided that we behave in a manner which corresponds to the revelation of this triumph.

Prayer has been very prominent in the first main part of this letter. It is not surprising, therefore, that Paul should exhort his readers to pray in this part (6:18-20). It is by prayer — itself a grace: "in the Spirit" (v.18) — that the Christians become and remain sensitive to fact that the "mystery" in which they are involved is not of their invention, that it originates with God and that it requires an openness on their part. If Paul has previously prayed for his readers (1:15-22; 3:1-19), he now enlists their prayers for himself, once again reminding them that his gospel — which is their salvation — comes not from himself but is God's word.

> [10]Finally, be strong in the Lord and in the strength of his might. [11]Put on the whole armor of God, that you may be able to stand against the wiles of the devil. [12]For we are not contending against flesh and blood, but against the principalities, against the powers, against the world rulers of this present darkness, against the spiritual hosts of wickedness in the heavenly places. [13]Therefore take the whole armor of God, that you may be able to withstand in the evil day, and having done all, to stand. [14]Stand therefore, having girded your loins with truth, and having put on the breastplate of righteousness, [15]and having shod your feet with the equipment of the gospel of peace; [16]above

all taking the shield of faith, with which you can quench all the flaming darts of the evil one. [17]And take the helmet of salvation, and the sword of the Spirit, which is the word of God. [18]Pray at all times in the Spirit, with all prayer and supplication. To that end keep alert with all perseverance, making supplication for all the saints, [19]and also for me, that utterance may be given me in opening my mouth boldly to proclaim the mystery of the gospel, [20]for which I am an ambassador in chains; that I may declare it boldly, as I ought to speak.

BE STRONG IN THE LORD.
6:10-17.

Paul's final exhortation is again addressed to all the faithful. The first part of it sounds like a rallying call to a battle. God's victory over his enemies is a biblical metaphor of salvation, and God (or the Messiah) is depicted in Jewish literature as a warrior armed for battle (Is 11:4-5; 59:16-18; Wis 5:17-23). The significance of the present exhortation is that it is the faithful who are to take up these arms. Paul has touched on this theme of the spiritual warfare in previous letters (1 Thes 5:8; 2 Cor 6:7; 10:3-4; Rom 13:12), but he has nowhere developed it as thoroughly as here. What makes this all the more striking is the fact that, in the first part of his "homily", Paul has insisted that "the battle is over", that is that God has already achieved our salvation in Christ. Now he appears to be saying that the battle is still to be won. This paradox is resolved by the consideration that salvation has indeed been accomplished radically in Christ. He has gained supremacy over all the forces inimical to God (1:21). Nevertheless, we have to make this victory our own and actually achieve our own salvation with God's armory.

The sectaries of Qumran envisaged the end of time as a huge battle between themselves (the sons of light) and God's enemies (the sons of darkness). Paul is doubtless alluding to this theme here. For Paul, however, the battle is entirely spiritual.

Warfare – even spiritual warfare – is not a metaphor that is very congenial to our modern mentality, especially when we realise that belligerent spiritual forces outside man are part of an outmoded cosmology. Nevertheless, once it is demythologised it can be seen to convey a message of perennial value. Far from remaining passive in face of God's initiative and immanent saving work, we can, and must, achieve salvation personally. The idea of conflict brings out this facet of salvation very well. It also suggests that we are not only the beneficiaries of salvation but also its instruments. As "other Christs" we have to continue Christ's Messianic work. By our baptism we not only "put on" Christ (4:24); we are also invested with his mission.

PRAY AT ALL TIMES IN THE SPIRIT.
6:18-20.

Finally, Paul exhorts his readers to pray. It is interesting and probably very significant that these last three verses do not form a sentence of their own but conclude the previous one in this way ". . . . which is the word of God,[18] with all prayer and supplication, praying at all times in the Spirit!" This *could* mean that it is precisely *through* prayer that the final eschatological battle is fought and won, that all the armory of the previous section is mobilised. However this may be, the exhortation to prayer certainly forms the climax to Paul's *cri de guerre*.

According to Paul, prayer is in fact a kind of "battle" not so much with external hostile force as with oneself (Rom 15:30). It is a struggle precisely because it involves opening oneself the action of the other that is God, seeing reality as he sees it, changing one's whole way of life accordingly. This is why it is possible only in the Spirit (Rom 8:26-27). As we have seen, however, this conflict is not only for one's own benefit; it is also for others. Thus it is above all by prayer that we become open to God's saving plan for the world and, like him, well disposed towards the rest of the universe. Real prayer engages not only our lips and our heart but our whole being. Our prayer for the salvation of the world is sincere only in so far as we really *want* it. This desire for the good of others does not come spontaneously. It is in fact the fruit of God's own love for the universe. It is a gift of God, but because of our radical selfishness we find it difficult to accept this gift. This is why prayer is so important and such a struggle or "agony" – even for Jesus (Lk 22:44). Paul exhorts his readers to such prayer "for all the saints" because he knows that this prayer, like the collection (1:15), will be an expression of their love and so be a binding force in the church (4:16).

In particular, Paul urges his readers to pray for the success of his apostolate (v.19). We have seen how important Paul's own personal prayer is in this work (1:15-16). Now he enlists the prayer of others, and from what he says here and elsewhere it is clear that he relies on this prayer (Rom 15:30-32; Col 4:3-4). He considers the apostolate to be a communal effort, the task of the whole church. The loving support which he has from his fellow "saints" enables him preach the gospel with increasing confidence and boldness (3:12).

There is something extremely refreshing and actual about this final exhortation of Paul. It reminds us of an element which often seems to be missing from much of contemporary theology: prayer, particularly intercessory prayer, "apostolic" prayer. Paul would be the first to concede both that there are different roles or functions (including the apostolate) within the church (4:7-16) and that the essence of the Christian life is a radically new behaviour in all the areas of human existence (4:17-6:9). But, permeating and inspiring all this, Paul sees that attitude of conscious attention or attentiveness to God's saving plan which he calls "prayer". This attitude of being transcends time, place and functions within the church. It is the prerogative and the duty of every "saint". Whoever and wherever we are, we can and must at all times be attentive to God and his saving plan. This is of the essence of Christianity.

NOTE:

Hope

According to Paul, the baptized already have access to God as Father: "for through him we both *have access* in one Spirit to the Father" (2:18). To this extent, therefore, they are already God's children and, being in his presence, are "holy" here and now. Nevertheless, the Holy Spirit is also given to them as a "*guarantee* of our inheritance *until we acquire possession* of it" (1:14; cf. also 4:30). Thus there is a futuristic aspect of the Christ-event. Salvation is given to us as an "inheritance", that is we have to await its future accomplishment. The "fulness of time" (1:10), which began with Christ, has not yet reached its term.

The God-given attitude which refers to this future dimension of Christian existence is hope. It is by faith that we receive the "gospel", by love that we realize and actualize it in the here and now, by hope that we tend towards its perfect fulfilment. Apart from a reference to the situation of the Jews prior to the advent of Christ (1:12), Paul does not mention the virtue of hope explicitly. But it is implicit in his presentation of complete salvaton as a future reality. In fact he refers to this salvation as a "hope": ". . . . that you may know the *hope* to which he has called you" (1:18; cf. 2:12; 4:4). This passage contains another important term which is linked with the idea of hope: "call". In presenting the "gospel" as a "call", Paul focuses its futuristic aspect: the "gospel" is continually inviting us to leave our present position and advance in our Christian life. This implies that our baptism is only an initiation into a new existence. We have to progress in this life. It is by hope that we are assured of our eventual success. This is because the same divine word which has made us God's children is now calling us. It is bound to produce its effect in us, provided that we welcome it by hope. Hope is to the future aspect of God's word what faith is to its present aspect.

Closely allied with the notion of call is that of "walking": "I . . . . beg you *to walk* in a manner worthy of the calling to which you have been called" (4:1). The R.S.V. naturally translates the verb "to walk" here by "to behave", because "to walk" is a well known semitism for "to behave". But the notion of walking is significant if for no other reason than that it suggests that we have somewhere to go, some distance to cover before we reach our final goal. It is a metaphor of hope. We know that if we "walk" in the "good works, which God prepared beforehand" (2:10) we are bound to reach our proper destiny.

Hope is also implied in all the intercessory prayers which Paul makes for his readers' salvation: "that you may *know* what is the hope to which he has called you, what are the riches of his glorious inheritance in the saints" (1:18). "To know" here does not mean merely to know about, that is to have an intellectual acquaintance with, our hope and inheritance. It means to experience, to enjoy. Paul is praying that his readers may reach final fulfilment (cf. also 3:14-19). If his readers are to enter into the spirit of his prayer, they must hope that it will be answered in their regard.

But perhaps the most poignant expression of the theme of hope in Ephesians is the metaphor of the "spiritual combat" (6:10-17). On the one hand, this image implies that the "walk" towards our final destination is by no means an easy one. On the contrary, it involves a struggle, a battle. The theme of the eschatological battle was current in the Judaism of Paul's day, especially in the writings of the Qumran sect. Paul here applies it to the lives of the faithful. The fact that there is going to be a battle, and this precisely with the very powers which Christ is supposed to have subdued (1:20-23), itself indicates that these powers are still dangerously active and have to be engaged. On the other hand, the faithful can be well armed for this battle. "Can be" is the operative phrase here, because Paul does not merely inform his readers that they are well armed. He *exhorts* them to be so. They have to "be strong", to "put on", to "take", to "stand" – all these are actions which the faithful themselves have to perform. Nevertheless, the armory in question is the "armor *of God*" (6:11), all of which is a detailed metaphor of "the strength of his might" (6:10; cf. 1:19). All of God's blessings: truth, righteousness, the gospel, faith, salvation, the Spirit, the word, previously presented as having been given to the faithful, now have to be "taken up" or "put on" actively and personally by the faithful. It is worth noting that all these blessings, with the exception of righteousness, figure in 1:13. Righteousness is mentioned in 4:24, but even here it is the righteousness *of truth*. The fact that these blessings are available to the faithful as a panoply is a guarantee of success in the battle against evil. Read properly, Paul's exhortation to moral armament is a message of hope. It reminds us that being a Christian involves a struggle, but it also assures us of the happy outcome of this struggle. The radical source of the Christian's hope is the final blessing of the Spirit which he received in baptism (1:13-14).

PERSONAL NEWS.
6:21-22.

²¹Now that you also may know how I am and what I am doing, Tychicus the beloved brother and faithful minister in the Lord will tell you everything. ²²I have sent him to you for this very purpose, that you may know how we are, and that he may encourage your hearts.

APART from the passing references to Paul's imprisonment (3:1,13; 4:1; 6:20), our letter is devoid of any personal news about Paul. Paul has confined himself to more important business. He is concerned, however, that his readers should have news of him. He is sending Tychicus for this purpose. It is probably Tychicus who actually bears the letter to the community.

FINAL GREETING.
6:23-24.

²³Peace be to the brethren, and love with faith, from God the Father and the Lord Jesus Christ. ²⁴Grace be with all who love our Lord Jesus Christ with love undying.

AFTER ALL that we have seen about prayer, it is impossible to regard this as a mere formal greeting (1:1-2). Paul is here praying that his readers may have the peace, love, faith and grace which have been the main subjects of his letter. But he cannot take leave of them without reminding them that these gifts demand their undying fidelity.

POSTWORD.

EPHESIANS IS RELEVANT to several interests of contemporary man. Paul here expresses more clearly and serenely than anywhere else the fact that God's plan for mankind involves the rest of creation. While man – the man Jesus and in Him all other men – remains the focal point of this plan, the whole cosmos – this world of ours – is also to be saved. In Ephesians Paul does not envisage an "end" to this world, in the sense of its destruction. Indeed the morality which he advocates is very much concerned with this world. It is not at all "other worldly". Precisely how the cosmos is to be saved is one of the most urgent questions of modern theology.

It is in the Church that the "fulness" of God, that is, God's plan for the cosmos, is revealed and should be realised. As Vatican II has pointed out, the Church is the sign and sacrament of salvation. The Church is called to be the revelation, the model and exemplar of God's plan for all men – and indeed for the whole cosmos. This fact – evident in Ephesians – presents a frightening challenge to any group (and Vatican II uses the term "Church" of at least eight different groups) which boasts of the name "Church". The challenge to the "catholic" church is particularly poignant, since Ephesians makes it clear that true universality is found in Christ, and that any absolute value given to anything that is not universally human is divisive: the Church is the new man. The task of the Church is to become – and to be seen to become – ever more human, after the model of Christ.

Christian morality is proper human behaviour, corresponding to God's revelation in Christ. The unique norm of human behaviour is Christ. The new life of the Christian, far from entailing his flight from the world, invades every area of his personal, social and family life. This is the "milieu" in which he lives and operates. The task of the Christian is to become what he already is by baptism: holy. This is the work of God within him, but he has to accept and welcome it actively.

Prayer is an essential part of the Christian life, as this is depicted in Ephesians. It is only by prayer – the prayer of intercession – that we become open to the activity of God within us and are thus able to lead a life worthy of our call. But prayer – the prayer of blessing, thanksgiving and praise – is the highest form of activity to which we are called. Ephesians reminds us of the intimate relationship between prayer and activity, between liturgy and life. Our prayer, our liturgy must be an expression of what we are called to be and are trying to be in Christ.

FURTHER READING

Both *The Jerome Biblical Commentary* and the *New Catholic Commentary on Holy Scripture* contain comprehensive introductions to Ephesians and a brief commentary on the text. They also provide a bibliography of more critical works up to the time of their publication (1968).

G.B. Caird *Paul's Letters from Prison*, (The New Clarendon Bible), Oxford University Press, 1976.

This is a brief, critical commentary, preceded by a very clear and balanced introduction.

J.L. Houlden *Paul's Letters from Prison*, (Pelican Commentary), S.C.M. 1977.

This is an excellent, up-to-date commentary, aimed at the general reader. The introduction, which gives a very balanced view of all the relevant questions, is particularly recommendable.

M. Barth, *Studies in Ephesians*, London: Mowbrays 1956.

This is a popular consideration of some of the major themes of Ephesians. It is a good introduction to the theology of the letter.

J.C. Kirby, *Ephesians, Baptism and Pentecost*, London: S.P.C.K. 1968.

A very interesting and illuminating study on the baptismal background of Ephesians. It also contains an excellent survey of the whole authorship debate.

P. Benoit, *Body, Head and Pleroma in the Letters of the Captivity*, in: *Jesus and the Gospel*, vol. 2, London: Darton, Longman & Todd 1974, pp. 51-92.

This a very interesting study, showing the importance of and the inter-relationship between these three major themes.